PRESERVED BUSES

VOLUME ONE

MUNICIPAL FLEETS

BY

JOHN A SENIOR MCIT

Venture *publications*

The municipal bus – In northern England as in many other parts of the country the Leyland-bodied PD1 or PD2 was typical of buses in many fleets. This Todmorden example, seen again on page 73, had just passed the now defunct Dinting Railway Centre, Glossop, when it was photographed on a glorious summer's day in the early 'seventies, running what would nowadays be called a heritage service.

CONTENTS

ISBN 1 898432 66 X © JA SENIOR JANUARY 1996

COMPUTERISED PRODUCTION FOR THE PUBLISHERS BY MOPOK GRAPHICS 128 PIKES LANE, GLOSSOP, DERBYSHIRE

FOREWORD

Preserved vehicles allow us to turn back the clock – to discover makes and types long since gone, or perhaps to rediscover almost forgotten memories from childhood. From April to October most weekends see gatherings of old buses at rallies held throughout the country and enthusiasts and families alike gather to marvel at the standard of workmanship which the vehicles recreate. Here, very often, is the opportunity to see just how things were done in the good old days. Paintwork with a mirror-like finish, beautifully lined in gold leaf and embellished with ornate corner motifs, set off by large gold numerals counter shaded in hues of blue and red – all signs of a distant age when the appearance of its fleet was part of the municipal pride in the transport department. The pictures in this book recall those days, and also provide some background information for those who wish to know a little more.

ACKNOWLEDGEMENTS

I would like to record my thanks to several people who have been particularly helpful in the compilation of this album, the first in a series intended to show the wide variety of vehicles which have been preserved and the magnificent standard of restoration achieved in so many cases.

Geoff Lumb has carried out the research to enable the captions to be put together in such a way as to provide a useful source of reference; Eric Ogden and Alan Townsin have checked the proofs and suggested improvements which we have been pleased to incorporate; John Robinson has kindly provided the photographs on pages 12, 13, 21, 25, 37, 38, 43, 45, 47, 63 and 73 to supplement my own collection and to assist in providing a wider spread of operators.

Finally, but my means least, I thank the many vehicle owners and drivers who have patiently posed their vehicles to allow the photographs to be taken. I hope the end result will please you all.

John A Senior
Simmondley

'All dressed up and nowhere to go' . . .

– just part of a long line of preserved double-decker buses awaiting inspection by the thousands of enthusiasts and other visitors who will see them at this typical rally event during May 1994.

The fascinating selection of makes, types, and liveries – mostly from their former owners – seen here provides a nostalgic and pleasant day out for everyone.

BUS PRESERVATION

Many people attending bus rallies marvel at the high standards of restoration achieved, not realising that very often the work has been carried out by the owner and one or two friends, probably none of whom are vehicle builders, and the restoration has perhaps been carried out in the open air over several years.

The old liveries and advertisements carried by the vehicles bring back many memories, but for those who wonder how it all happens, or how it began, a brief explanation will probably be of interest.

Unlike the railway companies which, in many cases, put examples of particularly interesting locomotives or rolling stock on one side for eventual preservation, the bus industry tended to get rid of its old vehicles when they were life expired.

Prior to 1960 there was, in any case, no national transport museum where they could be displayed and so, sadly, most went for scrap.

There are always exceptions, and London Transport had the resources to be able to afford to keep a good selection of representative vehicles dating back to pre-First World War days, but such dedication was unusual. Several operators had ancient vehicles dumped in dark corners of depots, sometimes seeing the light of day as tree loppers, or decorated for carnivals, but to spend time and money restoring them was pointless unless there was to be some very good reason, or somewhere to display them.

The determination of tramway enthusiasts to preserve a selection of old tramcars, and then in 1955 to form a society with the aim of creating a working tramway museum, did much to galvanise bus enthusiasts. And buses had the advantage that they were mobile, unlike the rail-bound tramcars.

Accordingly, forty years ago, in 1956, a letter appeared in *The Veteran and Vintage Magazine* suggesting that since car rallies and steam traction engine events held during the summer months were attracting large crowds, why shouldn't there be a commercial vehicle rally?

About the same time six London bus enthusiasts had persuaded London Transport to sell to them for preservation an elderly motor bus which had outlived all others of its type. This was a 1929 AEC Regal single-deck bus, registered UU 6646, with fleet number T31. These six enthusiasts joined forces under the title of the **Vintage Passenger Vehicle Society (VPVS)** to restore T31, and also to encourage like-minded would-be preservationists to purchase other vehicles of their own choice.

In July 1957 Lord Montague of Beaulieu made the rally idea possible – and put the seal of respectability on the movement by letting it be held in the beautiful grounds of Beaulieu Abbey. It was attended by 30 old commercial vehicles and such was the success of the event that it was followed in early 1958 by the formation of **The Historic Commercial Vehicle Club** with Lord Montague as President, and Sir William Black, Chairman of AEC/ACV, as Patron.

Rallies were held in 1958 at both Leyland and Southall, the homes of the industry's principal commercial and passenger chassis builders. The movement continued to expand with the formation in 1959 of the **Lincoln Vintage Vehicle Society**, which, like many other groups and individuals, targeted for purchase interesting elderly vehicles still in service. Many of these vehicles came from Jersey, for the island had become home to many old buses withdrawn from active service on the mainland and pensioned-off for a quieter life serving holiday makers in the Summer season.

By 1959 the tramway museum had become a reality – at Crich in Derbyshire – but a national transport museum was still only a pipe dream. London Transport hoped to be able to display its old vehicles

Taking a vintage bus for an outing has the advantage that you can take your friends along too. Some people hire such vehicles to take wedding parties to the reception. Here the famous London General T-type mentioned above pauses for a moment before giving a demonstration run to the sponsors of one of the rally events. Many years of work were needed to restore it to original condition.

at a national museum planned by the British Transport Commission, and this eventually came about in 1963 at the former Clapham bus garage. Sadly it closed only ten years later as part of the policy to move certain museums from London to the provinces. Although selected railway exhibits found a home in the enlarged National Railway Museum at York, and the London bus, tram and trolleybus exhibits spent six years at Syon Park before going to their present home at Covent Garden, London, many of the other buses were placed in store where some remain to this day.

In 1962 the **VPVS** and the **London Vintage Taxi Club** joined forces with the **HCVC** to form one major club catering for all forms of commercial vehicles. Also in 1962 the enlarged HCVC started its annual London to Brighton run for commercial vehicles, which is still held on the first Sunday in May each year and does much to foster enthusiasm in the preservation movement.

One municipality proud of its past heritage was Portsmouth, which had kept examples of a former horse tram converted to electric propulsion, together with an early motor bus, and had also kept its first trolleybus, No. 201. The latter was then loaned for

display in the early 1960s at the Beaulieu Motor Museum together with a tramcar from Newcastle-on-Tyne, owned by the **Tramway Museum Society** but without a suitable home at that time.

Practically every preservation project involving motor buses has been faced with accommodation problems, double-deckers being a particular difficulty, and the HCVC planned its own museum to display the vehicles which the Club had acquired. In the meantime many of these buses were stored in a building erected at Carlton Colville, near Lowestoft, Suffolk, on the site being developed as the **East Anglia Transport Museum**.

As the number of buses purchased for preservation grew, more vintage vehicle rallies began to be held at weekends. Geoff Lumb recalls going to one in Rochdale, in September 1967, where nine commercial vehicles and buses were displayed for the afternoon in a local park. His entry collected the award for travelling the furthest distance to the event – all of fifteen miles from Huddersfield. Today a vehicle winning such an award is likely to have travelled two hundred miles or more.

As the movement grew, more events were arranged by clubs, societies or individuals, and many of these

have become annual occasions. In some cases the local authority organised them to coincide with civic celebrations.

Many of these rallies involved a road run before the vehicles were placed on display to the public with entrants competing against each other for the honour of having the best vehicle at the rally, or the best in a particular class. It also became common practice for the entrant to receive an attendance plaque as a souvenir of the event.

One of the founder members of the VPVS, Prince J. Marshall, had become one of the Vice Presidents of the HCVC after the merger of both societies. Prince promoted the movement further in 1962 when he launched two new magazines – *Old Motor* and *Vintage Commercial* to cater for people interested in old vehicles. Eventually both magazines were merged under the *Old Motor* title.

A keen supporter of historic vehicle rallies, Prince organised several including the highly successful 'Grand Transport Extravaganza' held at the Crich Tramway Museum on August Bank Holiday weekends for many years.

He believed that vehicles should be preserved as working examples, rather than being over-restored

Left: This is what many old buses look like before they are rescued. Here a former Ashton-under-Lyne three-axle Karrier bus finishes its days as a caravan before being taken to the Golcar Transport Collection for restoration.

Right: Gently does it! Some vehicles can be driven away, others are taken to their new homes on the end of a tow-bar; most old timers go this way. Modern requirements for Health and Safety, together with increased volumes of traffic on the roads, require professional means of removal to be employed. Someone will have the important job of driving behind to keep an eye on things.

polished-show-pieces, and restored his 1930 former 'Tilling' ST-type accordingly. Such was the standard achieved that a 'certificate of fitness' – enabling it to be used in revenue service – was granted. He then persuaded London Transport to hire the vehicle and to place it back into service on a special 'Vintage Bus Service'. This was quite an achievement for a vehicle which had been in a scrap yard for fourteen years before being rescued in 1966.

The preservation movement suffered a great loss when Prince Marshall died in hospital on 14th November 1981, aged 43. He left a movement which has grown year by year, with the establishment of many museums and collections such as the **London Bus Preservation Trust** at Cobham whose members occupy premises built in the Second World War by Vickers Ltd to construct wing sections for Wellington bombers —and believed to have been the experimental base from which Barnes Wallis developed his 'bouncing bomb' for the RAF Dambusters.

Amongst many other museums deserving mention are the **Museum of Transport**, Manchester established in 1979 to house the vehicles which were collected from 1970 when the **SELNEC Society** was formed, the Aston Manor Museum in the Midlands and the Wythall Museum, also in the Midlands. More recently in Scotland new premises were acquired in 1995 at Lathalmond, near Dunfermline, Fife, to house the **Scottish Vintage Bus Museum**'s collection of over 100 buses. This includes examples from municipalities, the former Scottish Bus Group and independents as well as BET, and Tilling fleets.

Prince Marshall's pioneering use of a vintage bus in service has been followed by many more. They include the use of vintage buses on free bus services at many transport rallies, such as the **Heart of the Pennines Bus Rally** held in Halifax which is organised by Tony Blackman and other members of the **Mersey and Calder Bus Preservation Group**. This enables many passengers and spectators to enjoy seeing old vehicles in use whilst also having the opportunity to ride on some of them.

This is the background to the Bus Preservation movement, but it is only the beginning of many thousands of stories involving dedication, financial problems and many hours of hard work necessary to rebuild a vehicle to working order. Most owners are only too pleased to talk about their projects and many people have become involved in restoration projects from casual conversations with proud owners of vehicles like the ones shown in this album.

Left: Prince Marshall's ST-type, operating on everyday service in London, proved what could be done when enthusiasts worked with the bus operators. It also demonstrated the value of such exercises, not only in Public Relations but also in revenue terms. Maintained in first-class condition by Tim Nicholson, it had no difficulty in keeping up with modern traffic.

Right: Preservation at work. Geoff Lumb's well-known Llandudno Guy, strategically parked for maximum effect, is on home ground in Llandudno some twenty years after it was withdrawn from service on this very route. Down below, the skipper of PS Waverley, the last ocean going paddle-steamer in the world, steers a course to Llandudno's pier, comfortably passing the headland despite the impression the camera gives.

THE MUNICIPAL BUS

The operation of public transport by local authorities was commonplace in the United Kingdom, some 117 having been involved at one time or another in the provision of transport for the local populace when the effects of bus deregulation caused the system to change, in 1986.

The first form of local transport, as opposed to the long distance stage coach, was often the horse tramway. As mechanised forms of propulsion became more reliable, various alternatives were sought, since the horse was an expensive form of motive power to operate and maintain, and also one which had difficulty in coping with steep gradients.

Parliamentary approval was necessary before a tramway could be constructed, but the actual operation had to be carried out by private enterprise. In only one instance did it prove impossible to find a company willing to take the risk, Huddersfield being so hilly that the problems were considered to be sufficient to eliminate any possibility of operating profitably.

In all other cases the local authority leased the lines to the operator, retaining the right to take over the system after 21 years. For this reason most local authorities became operators of their local transport around the turn of the century, after the 21 years of company operation, if their town had had a tramway.

Towns which started with electric trams were able to avoid this problem by applying for Parliamentary approval for local authority operation. Similarly, authorities wanting to go straight into bus operation had to apply for Parliamentary powers to do so.

Thus the municipal operators came into being, and with relatively few changes remained in existence until the events of 1986. The success of many of these municipalities in producing a substantial operating surplus to plough back in to the authority's rate fund was impressive, thereby reducing the amount payable by local rates, but as local transport patronage declined in the 1960s so the economics began to be loaded against the small operator.

Some coped very well, and when the PTEs were set up from 1969 it was a bone of contention that not always was there an improvement in service, value for money or standard of vehicle turnout.

The question of vehicle appearance was always a key one for the municipalities, and many and varied were the liveries employed. The question of municipal pride was usually at the top of the agenda and the transfer of a municipal fleet to a PTE or other operator was seen as a great loss to the local community.

An advantage when local authorities had control over their own affairs was the opportunity to support local industry. As the end of the twentieth century approaches it is easy to forget that 50 years ago operators had a wide choice of manufacturers with whom to negotiate for their vehicles, and many authorities could select a local company. Thus Coventry supported Daimler, and Manchester supported Crossley, to take two well-known examples.

Those who advocate large scale enterprise will point out that there are so few manufacturers left nowadays that the question of local autonomy is academic; others will remember when freedom of choice meant that greater individuality could be achieved without sacrificing efficiency.

The photographs in this book will evoke instant nostalgia for those who remember municipal buses, whilst the captions and tables will hopefully answer questions which many people will ask when they see the vehicles at rallies, or as they read this book. Only two of the former municipalities are not represented by a preserved vehicle – Stockton and Colwyn Bay.

The table overleaf shows the state of the municipal bus fleets from the 1974 boundary changes onwards. The second volume of *Preserved Municipal Buses* will provide a detailed list of all the municipalities, together with details of the types of vehicles they operated: tram, trolley or motor bus.

The municipal bus carried its local authority's crest, usually boldly emblazoned on the side panels. Where four authorities were involved the coat-of-arms could be quite complex, as here with SHMD, (see page 63).

There is absolutely no doubt as to who owns the vehicle on which this coat-or-arms is displayed. Gold leaf was commonly used and some of the styles remained unchanged from tramway days in smaller fleets.

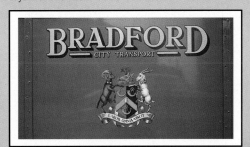

Only the 'legal lettering' which every psv had to display in letters 1in high on its nearside panelling would reveal that a bus carrying this crest actually came from Haslingden, in Lancashire.

British Municipal Undertakings Since 1974

Status c1974-85	1985 Status	Subsequent Changes in Ownership
Aberconwy Borough Council	Extant	
Barrow-in-Furness Corporation Transport		No longer trading
Blackburn Borough Transport Department	Blackburn Borough Transport Ltd (*)	
Blackpool Borough Council Transport Department	Blackpool Transport Services Ltd (*)	
Bournemouth Transport	Bournemouth Transport Ltd (*)	
Brighton Borough Transport	Brighton Borough Transport Ltd	MEBO (Management Employee Buyout)
Burnley & Pendle Joint Transport	Burnley & Pendle Transport Co Ltd (*)	
City of Cardiff Transport	Cardiff City Transport Services Ltd (*)	
Chester City Transport	Chester City Transport Ltd (*)	
Chesterfield (Borough of) Transport Department	Chesterfield Transport Ltd	MBO then to Stagecoach Holdings plc
Cleveland Transit	Cleveland Transit Ltd	MEBO then to Stagecoach Holdings plc
(Langbaurgh, Middlesbrough & Stockton-on-Tees Joint Transport Committee)		
Colchester Borough Transport	Colchester Borough Transport Ltd	To British Bus Group plc
Colwyn Borough Council		No longer trading
Cynon Valley Borough Council Transport Department	Cynon Valley Transport Ltd	No longer trading
Darlington (Borough of) Transport Department	Darlington Transport Co Ltd	No longer trading
Derby City Transport	Derby City Transport Ltd	To British Bus Group plc
Douglas Corporation Transport Department	Since 1976 horse trams only	Buses to Isle of Man National Transport Ltd
Eastbourne Borough Council Transport Department	Eastbourne Buses Ltd (*)	
East Staffordshire District Council Transport Department		Sold to Stevenson, Uttoxeter then to British Bus Group plc No longer trading
Fylde Borough Council Transport	Fylde Borough Transport Ltd	To Blackpool Transport
Grampian Regional Council Department Public Transport	Grampian Regional Transport Ltd	GRT Holdings plc then to First Bus plc
Great Yarmouth Borough Council Transport Department	Great Yarmouth Transport Ltd (*)	
Grimsby & Cleethorpes Joint Transport Committee	Grimsby-Cleethorpes Transport Co Ltd	To Stagecoach Holdings plc
Halton (Borough of) Transport	Halton Borough Transport Ltd (*)	
Hartlepool Borough Transport Department	Hartlepool Transport Ltd	MEBO then to Stagecoach Holdings plc
Hyndburn (Borough of) Transport Department	Hyndburn Transport Ltd (*)	
Ipswich Borough Transport	Ipswich Buses Ltd (*)	
Islwyn Borough Council Transport Department	Islwyn Borough Transport Ltd (*)	
Kingston-upon-Hull City Transport Department	Kingston-upon-Hull City Transport Ltd	To Cleveland Transit Ltd then to Stagecoach Holdings plc

British Municipal Undertakings Since 1974

Status c1974-85	1985 Status	Subsequent Changes in Ownership
Lancaster City Council Passenger Transport Dept	Lancaster City Transport Ltd	No longer trading
Leicester City Transport	Leicester Citybus Ltd	To GRT Holdings plc then toFirst Bus plc
Lincoln City Transport	Lincoln City Transport Ltd	To Yorkshire Traction Company Ltd
Lothian Regional Transport	Lothian Region Transport Ltd (*)	
Maidstone Borough Council Transport Department	Maidstone Borough Transport (Holdings) Ltd	
		No longer trading
Merthyr Tydfil Borough Council Passenger Transport Department		No longer trading
Newport Borough Transport	Newport Transport Ltd (*)	
Northampton Transport	Northampton Transport Ltd	To GRT Holdings then toFirst Bus plc
Nottingham (City of) Transport	Nottingham City Transport Ltd (*)	
Plymouth City Transport	Plymouth Citybus Ltd (*)	
Portsmouth City Transport	Portsmouth City Transport Ltd	To Transit Holdings Ltd
Preston (Borough of) Transport Department	Preston Borough Transport Ltd	MEBO
Reading Transport	Reading Transport Ltd (*)	
Rhymney Valley District Council Transport Dept	Inter-Valley Link Ltd	No longer trading
Rossendale Transport	Rossendale Transport Ltd (*)	
Southampton City Transport	Southampton City Transport Co Ltd	Employees
Southend Transport	Southend Transport Ltd	To British Bus Group plc
Taff-Ely Borough Council Transport Department	Taff-Ely Transport Ltd	No longer trading
Tayside Regional Council Transport Department	Tayside Public Transport Co Ltd	MEBO
Thamesdown Transport	Thamesdown Transport Ltd (*)	
Warrington Borough Council Transport Department	Warrington Borough Transport Ltd (*)	
Waveney District Council		Ceased to operate on 3/12/ 1977

Note that those municipal undertakings which became part of the Passenger Transport Executives between 1969 and 1974 do not appear in this list.

Aberconwy Borough Council is the only continuing municipality. The shares of the remaining 20 companies, marked (*), are held by the Local Authority concerned (at January 1996).

JOJ 489

CHASSIS	CROSSLEY DD42/7	1950
BODY	CROSSLEY	1950
TYPE	54-SEAT REAR ENTRANCE	

Preserved vehicles from big city fleets always attract attention at rallies, often because so many people will have encountered them in daily travel to work in days gone by. Birmingham is well represented and this example is a credit to its owners.

In 1950 Birmingham City Transport took delivery of its final batch of Crossley double-deck buses fitted with 54-seat Crossley bodies, built to Birmingham specification. The earlier design used for the first 170 Crossleys was tidied up and the last 100 of the type, Nos. 2426 to 2525, had a new front-end design, evolved by BCT in co-operation with its suppliers, called the 'new look', a name then in use for the latest feminine fashion trend.

All BCT's further purchases of what were then conventional half-cab double-deck buses would incorporate the new look front which concealed the manufacturer's radiator. This new front was a steel pressing which meant that buses built by Crossley, Daimler and Guy all looked the same to the average passenger, especially when wheel discs were fitted, further disguising any distinguishing features. It was offered to other operators and a number bought AECs with the same new look front.

Number 2489, fitted with a Crossley type 7/5B engine, was withdrawn in March 1969. The bus was built with 30 seats in the upper deck but due to the fitting of the Birmingham pattern of straight safety staircase only 24 passengers were accommodated in the lower saloon.

It was placed into store and in late September 1969 was bought by an individual from BCT before being collected on 4th October. West Midlands PTE had taken over the Black Country municipal buses of Birmingham, Walsall, West Bromwich, and Wolverhampton on 1st October.

Number 2489 has been rallied every year since 1970 by the '2489 Group' and is kept in the West Midlands. In 1989 it was recertified as a PCV, obtaining a Class 6 certificate, and most people now affectionately know it as 'David Harvey's Crossley'. It was photographed at the Cobham event in April 1995.

Notice in the rear views, opposite, the cutaway rear, required by law to enable passengers to escape in the event of a bus falling on to its nearside. This is in addition to the rear upper-deck emergency exit.

BCB 340

CHASSIS	LEYLAND PS1	1948
BODY	CROSSLEY	1948
TYPE	32-SEAT FORWARD ENTRANCE	

Blackburn Corporation Transport did not introduce motor buses until 1929, 30 years after it commenced to operate electric tramcars. Its initial motor bus fleet comprised Leyland single and double-deck buses with Leyland built bodies and similar vehicles were supplied up to 1935, when two English Electric-bodied Leyland double-deck buses arrived. After further Leyland-bodied Leylands in 1935-38 two AEC double-deck buses with East Lancashire Coachbuilders bodies arrived in 1939 .

Wartime allocations included eleven Guy Arabs but with the return to peace ten Leyland PS1 single-deck buses with front entrance Crossley 32-seat bodies arrived in 1947-8 to replace the last of the pre-war single-deck fleet. One of these was No. 7, BCB 340, which arrived in March 1948 and was not withdrawn until the end of March 1967.

In March 1968 it was sold to D. W. Wright, organiser of a Manchester Boys Band. During the next few years it made two tours of the continent. Disused by 1972 it was bought for the sum of £210 for preservation by a group of four, calling themselves Blackburn No. 7 Preservation Society. The bus, a vandalised wreck, was rebuilt between 1976 and 1983, the group spending some £3,000 restoring the vehicle themselves. By 1985 the four active members had spent over £6,000 on a restoration which by any standards was excellent.

In 1988 No. 7 was returned on loan to Blackburn Transport Ltd, the successor to the Corporation, with ownership subsequently being transferred to the company.

It is seen in Southport during a rally in 1986 and its gleaming paintwork speaks volumes for the standard of workmanship achieved. Note the opening front windscreen, and sliding door.

The glazing of the windows, using rubber gaskets, whilst correct, is not to the original as-new specification. It was a modification introduced by many operators.

CHASSIS	GUY ARAB III	1949
BODY	CROSSLEY	1949
TYPE	56-SEAT REAR ENTRANCE	

When Blackburn Corporation finally abandoned its electric tramcars on 3rd September 1949 the replacing motor buses used were 20 Guy Arab IIIs with 6LW Gardner engines, the wartime Arabs clearly having found favour. The Arab IIIs carried Crossley 56-seat highbridge double-deck bus bodies, fleet numbers 120 to 139, CBV 420-439 and two of these – Nos. 131 and 133 – have survived into preservation.

The small windows at the rear of each saloon were a feature found on many Crossley bodies at this time, due to the method of bracing the structure to support the rear platform. As with the PS1 shown opposite, the side windows were reglazed in the course of a subsequent rebuild.

Number 133, new in August 1949, was sold after withdrawal in October 1972 to J. Dickenson, West Houghton and was kept at Bury Transport Museum. In March 1978 it changed hands again, this time to S. Spencer of Rawtenstall, a member of the East Lancashire Transport Preservation Group and was kept at Crawshawbooth and Edenfield at various dates.

In May 1987 it was again sold, this time to P. K. Historic Omnibus Co, Hunmanby, North Yorkshire. After the failure of PK it went to the Barnsley dealer, J. Sykes, in August 1988 and during September 1988 was taken into care by Ray Butcher, from East Didsbury, Manchester. Continuing to change carers by September 1990 it was being rallied by Adams from Stockton Brook. In 1991 it was in the ownership of G. Turner, Leek, Staffordshire and by September 1995 it had moved again, this time to Haynes of Stoke-on-Trent.

This series of moves provides a good example of the complex life many vehicles lead in preservation and much credit is due to those who struggle to keep examples of significant vehicles safe for posterity.

The other example mentioned, number 131, is in the St Helens Transport Museum requiring a full restoration.

FBN 232C

CHASSIS	LEYLAND PDR1/1	1965
BODY	EAST LANCS	1965
TYPE	78-SEAT FRONT ENTRANCE	

This stylish vehicle was one of 102 examples of the rear-engined Leyland Atlantean PDR1/1 buses built for Bolton in the period 1963-1968 and fitted with bodies by East Lancashire Coachbuilders of Blackburn (as here), Metro-Cammell of Birmingham or Neepsend Coachbuilders, the Sheffield subsidiary of East Lancs.

This large batch carried Bolton fleet Nos. 185-286 which later became SELNEC 6685-6786 after Bolton buses passed to the newly formed PTE in 1969. Unpopular with engineers when first introduced, the rear-engined chassis layout soon became the industry standard, allowing operation by one person who could drive the vehicle and collect the fares after changes in legislation which had previously restricted this to single deck vehicles only.

One of the batch, No. 6732, new in October 1965 as Bolton 232, was withdrawn in February 1979 by Greater Manchester PTE, successor to SELNEC. It was sold via Lister, the Bolton dealer, to the Ribble Vehicle Preservation Group in March 1979. Members of the Group restored it into original Bolton Corporation livery and from mid-1980 it was kept at Lonsdale Coaches premises in Heysham until it was acquired by P. Smalley and the Bolton Transport Group in November 1983 and moved to the Bolton Transport Museum. There it was repainted under a Manpower Services Commission scheme which saw a variety of buses and three trams restored or refurbished. Bolton Corporation buses had followed the same colour scheme as the trams, a dark maroon, until manager Ralph Bennett initiated ideas to attract passengers onto the buses, including a brighter revised livery as seen here. His interest in styling, of which this is an early example, was later seen to good effect in Manchester and, later, London.

In August 1993 ownership of No. 232 changed again when it passed into the care of the Bolton Bus Group. It is seen loading at the Halifax Piece Hall in 1995 and many of its passengers will be too young to remember any type of double-deck bus other than the rear-engined variety.

RRU 904

CHASSIS	LEYLAND PSUC1/1	1955
BODY	PARK ROYAL	1955
TYPE	42-SEAT FRONT ENTRANCE	

Bournemouth's very attractive colour scheme was a credit to the undertaking and very much a part of the town's up-market image. Any preserved vehicles carrying that livery will always stand out from other smart but perhaps less eye-catching colours and this spendidly restored single-decker is just such a case in point.

Single-deck bus chassis built in the 'fifties started the move to create more space for passengers by putting the engine beneath the floor. Leyland's first model was the Royal Tiger but soon a lighter weight version was developed, the famous Tiger Cub, which was in production from 1952 to 1962. It was popular with both bus and coach operators. This Leyland Tiger Cub model PSUC1/1, new in October 1955, was fitted with a Park Royal 41-seat dual-entrance body, reflecting Bournemouth's fondness for two-door bodywork, and was numbered 267 in the Corporation fleet. The translucent curved roof panels allowed holidaymakers to enjoy the Summer sunshine. It was later converted to a 42-seat front-entrance vehicle, being renumbered in 1958 as number 99. Park Royal bodywork was becoming less common on Leyland chassis when the vehicle was new, reflecting the link between PRV and AEC and its influence on customers.

Withdrawn from service in April 1971 it was one of four Bournemouth Tiger Cubs sold the following month to Burton-upon-Trent Corporation. Burton introduced one-man-operated buses into the town in June 1971. Number 99 was the last of the former Bournemouth vehicles to be placed in service, in May 1972, as fleet No. 4.

Following Local Government Reorganisation on 1st April 1974 Burton Corporation's motor buses came under the control of the East Staffordshire District Council and in May 1976 the bus was renumbered 24. After withdrawal from service it was sold in February 1978 to the Bournemouth Passenger Transport Association for preservation. This group had also bought the other three ex-Bournemouth vehicles in March 1977. Because of its duplication in the BPTA collection it was sold in 1991 to D. J. Griffiths from Southampton for continued preservation.

The former Bournemouth livery is shown to good advantage as the bus waits to enter the rally site at Netley Park, Southampton, on a glorious Sunday morning in July 1994. Many of the vehicles preserved by the BPTA have been restored to their original pristine condition for display at the Bournemouth Transport Museum. These include former Corporation buses and trolleybuses and an open-top tramcar which, after being withdrawn in Bournemouth, operated in very different terrain for the Llandudno and Colwyn Bay Electric Railway until that system closed in 1956. It then spent some time in the erstwhile Museum of Transport at Clapham before returning to Bournemouth.

HKW 82

CHASSIS	AEC REGENT III	1953
BODY	EAST LANCS	1953
TYPE	59-SEAT REAR ENTRANCE	

The casual observer often has no way of knowing just how much, or how little, major reconstruction has been necessary to bring a vehicle to the condition in which it is displayed. This is a very important point for judges at rallies when vehicles are assessed for the prizes. This immaculate example from Bradford is an example of a vehicle brought back from dereliction, though no one would think so.

It was one of 40 AEC Regent III type 9613E buses fitted with pre-selective transmission, fleet Nos. 66 to 105, which entered service between November 1952 and September 1953. Built to a very high overall specification they were fitted with attractive 59-seat East Lancashire Coachbuilders 8ft-wide bodies, and incorporated the Birmingham new-look front and bonnet which concealed the radiator. Their appearance was further enhanced by the fitting of wheel trims. In 1957 an additional double seat was fitted increasing the seating capacity upstairs from 33 to 35. These buses were withdrawn from service between August 1966 and the end of July 1972.

Number 82, new in 1952 and withdrawn from service in September 1971, was converted into a mobile generator bus to provide DC power to move trolleybuses in Thornbury works when the miners' strike caused power cuts in February and March 1972. This disrupted the use of trolleybuses for four weeks shortly before Bradford ceased operation of its 'silent servants'.

Number 82 survived, still with generator, to be taken over by the West Yorkshire PTE in 1974. Around 1977 it was sold in this form to provide emergency power at the Sandtoft Trolleybus Museum. Eventually, after removal of its mechanical units, it became the mess room for the Reading group, ownership being transferred in 1981 to the British Trolleybus Society.

In 1991 the remains of No. 82 were bought by Jim Speed who, with Darren Hunt, moved the remains away from Sandoft. The vehicle was then completely rebuilt, work which involved the replacement of most of the corroded steel framing for the body, even to the extent of having to fabricate new bulkheads, as well as finding a replacement engine and gearbox. Eventually No. 82 reappeared in the immaculate condition which befitted one of the fleet which was the pride and joy of Manager Chaceley Humpidge and which cost £4,507 14s. 2d. in 1952. A modern double-deck bus in 1996 will cost some £120,000.

6220 KW

CHASSIS	AEC REGENT V	1964
BODY	MCW	1964
TYPE	70-SEAT FORWARD ENTRANCE	

Typical of late 'fifties bus design is another example from Bradford. The traditional open rear platform seen opposite has given way to a later design in which the entrance was moved forward. Whilst many passengers would miss the opportunity to hop on-and-off at will such actions were clearly a traffic hazard and the new layout made for improved safety. The doors also allowed the bus to be kept warmer, there being little point in fitting bus heaters if all the heat was then allowed to escape via the open platform.

Between 1959 and 1964 Bradford City Transport placed 120 similar AEC Regent V double-deck motor buses into service and all were fitted with forward-entrance 70-seat Metropolitan-Cammell bodies, similar in style to that manufacturer's lightweight 'Orion' bodies seen operating in many parts of the country. Number 220 was one of 100 with synchromesh gearboxes.

Bradford's examples were heavier and better finished than many apparently similar vehicles and certainly compared favourably with the rather spartan examples supplied to Hebble Motor Services Ltd. Both types were used on the route to Huddersfield, jointly operated by Bradford, Hebble and Huddersfield JOC.

When the West Yorkshire PTE took over the Bradford fleet in April 1974, 115 of these buses were still in service. Number 220, 6220 KW, one of the last 30 to be bought, was withdrawn in 1975 and was then used by the PTE until 1982 as a mobile painters' mess room.

In 1985 it was acquired by the West Yorkshire Transport Museum and was restored into the smart Southsea blue and broken white Bradford livery.

It is now displayed and used at Transperience, the West Yorkshire Transport Discovery Park, which opened at Low Moor, Bradford in July 1995.

Also photographed at the AEC Rally held in Nottingham, this time in May 1994, the smart livery is a reminder that Bradford trolleybuses and buses were always immaculate, and were a credit to a city which, like many, operated its transport department with great municipal pride.

GHT 154

CHASSIS	**BRISTOL K5G**	**1940**
BODY	**BRISTOL (BRISLINGTON)**	**1940**
TYPE	**56-SEAT REAR ENTRANCE**	

This distinctive bus, with its weird profile, can rightly claim to have been home made, though two different companies were involved in its construction. The chassis was built by the Motor Constructional Works (MCW), a company based at Brislington after its move from Filton. After a long and varied career it became Bristol Commercial Vehicles and eventually passed into Leyland control in 1967 before being closed in 1984. The bodywork on this vehicle was built by the Brislington Works, part of the Bristol organisation, located at Brislington in the city's suburbs. The bodyworks operated from 1907 to 1955, supplying a wide variety of customers throughout the country.

GHT 154 was purchased to operate in its native city by Bristol Joint Services, an organisation formed in 1937 as a joint Bristol Corporation and Bristol Tramways & Carriage Co arrangement to co-ordinate transport in the city and share net revenue.

Trams had been the principal mode of transport in the city from 1875 and between 1895 and the end of 1900 the tramway company replaced all its horse trams with electric tramcars; these operated on twelve routes. The company never modernised the system, which at its maximum had

237 open-top tramcars, since it could have been compulsorily acquired by Bristol Corporation after every seven years.

An agreement, implemented after an Act of Parliament 'Bristol Transport Act 1937', allowed the Corporation to purchase the tramways on 1st October 1937 for £1,125,000, and then jointly with the Tramway Co to replace the last fleet of open-top tramcars with 272 Bristol K5G double-deck motor buses, most of these having 56-seat bodies built in the Bristol Tramways own bodyshops.

The Tramways company charged the 'joint services' the same price as it would charge any Thomas Tilling Ltd company – a price equal to the cost of production (including overhead expenses) of such vehicle or equipment plus ten per cent of such cost. The bus bodies and the chassis purchased were manufactured 'in-house', the chassis being fitted with a five-cylinder Gardner diesel engine with the high radiator so characteristic of pre-war Bristols. The Bristol Joint fleet, like the rest of the BTCC vehicles until c1944, was painted dark blue and white, displaying the Bristol coat of arms, and the buses were given a prefix 'C' for city. The county bus routes operated by the Tramway Company employed a separate fleet.

The tramway system was effectively closed by the Luftwaffe in the 1941 blitz on the city when the main power cable was cut by a bomb which fell at Bedminster.

One of the 'City' fleet, No. C3336, GHT 154 built in 1940, was withdrawn from service in 1953 and then spent nearly 20 years with a travelling showman who spent the winters at Taunton. Whilst with the showman the bus had its roof and staircase removed, becoming effectively a van, but with greater mobilty and without the fear of damage through fouling low railway bridges.

It was bought in 1972 by Colin Shears, for the West of England Transport collection at Winkleigh in north Devon. In May 1973 it was bought for preservation, being restored in an open yard using parts from a similar bus. The task was completed in 1982 with final repainting into the distinctive pre-war blue livery. The finished vehicle is now in the care of the Bristol Vintage Bus Group and was photographed in August 1994 and again in August 1995, on home ground at the Bristol Festival of Transport where it always delights Bristolians who still have fond memories of the blue and white buses and trams.

Bury Corporation operated electric tramcars from 3rd June 1903 until 13th February 1949. An unusual feature was the operation by the Corporation of the Radcliffe UDC and most of the Heywood Corporation tramway systems. All tramcar services except one – Tottington to Walmersley – had been withdrawn by 1938, but wartime pressures forced the reinstatement of the Manchester Road route. The original livery was red with pale cream relief but this had been replaced by the green and cream shown by the 'fifties.

Buses had been introduced in September 1925 and Bury was one of the Lancashire municipalities to operate jointly a long-distance express service, in this case from Bury to Stockport. In the 'thirties Daimler, Leyland, AEC and Crossley buses were purchased and Bury was one of the few to operate the Leyland 3-axle Titanic model.

Leyland became the favoured chassis make, though not exclusively so, with bodies built by Roe, Northern Counties and Weymann. Two AEC Regent III models were purchased, one of which survives in preservation, and more unusually two small Barnard-bodied Guys, identical to vehicles supplied to Llandudno and Colwyn Bay, were also purchased.

After spending its later years with SELNEC and then GMT, number 210 was withdrawn in January 1975 and sold to a lady preservationist, now Mrs Stephenson, who was a member of the Transport Appreciation Society. By 1987 her vehicle was being kept at the Bury Transport Museum, moving to the St Helens Transport Museum in May 1992.

It was photographed at Kidderminster Severn Valley Railway Station in Autumn 1995.

GEN 201

CHASSIS	LEYLAND TITAN PD3	1958
BODY	MCW	1958
TYPE	73-SEAT REAR ENTRANCE	

This fine vehicle, one of a batch of 20, represents the ultimate development of the front-engined, rear-entrance double-decker. Built for Bury in 1958, its specification took advantage of the then newly revised Construction and Use Regulations (see page 80), being constructed to 30ft long, thereby providing accommodation for 73 seated passengers. Platform doors are fitted, by no means universal even at that time. Only the movement of the entrance/exit to a forward position would improve on this basic concept of a reliable and well-tried design, easy to maintain and capable of giving trouble-free service day-in and day-out.

Part of the attraction of old vehicles usually lies in the splendid liveries they carry. The quality of the paintwork, gleaming and pristine, often with gold lining and large shaded numerals, has an appeal all of its own. During the Second World War many vehicles were painted in drab grey, due to the non-availability of pigments to manufacture traditional colours. Some operators with good paint stocks were able to repaint to peacetime standards, though with grey roofs to make buses less easily spotted from the air.

Most bodybuilders delivered new buses in various shades of grey from about 1942.

Cardiff Corporation commenced operating electric tramcar services in 1902 when it took over the routes worked by two horse tramway companies. The tramways were in turn replaced between 1942 and 1950 by trolleybuses until 1962 when the first route was converted to motor buses.

The first trolleybuses to be delivered to Cardiff had been ordered from Leyland Motors but due to Government restrictions on vehicle manufacture in the Second World War the order was transferred to AEC. The three axle chassis were fitted with English Electric equipment and Northern Counties, whose head office was located in Cardiff, built the attractively styled bodies in its Wigan works.

These 70-seat bodies were equipped for pay-as-you-enter operation, passengers paying the seated conductor the penny fare as they entered the vehicle. New in 1942, number 203 was withdrawn in March 1963. Cardiff's last trolleybus ran on 11th January 1970.

After withdrawal it was purchased by the Reading Transport Society and in 1970 ownership passed to the London Trolleybus Society, the vehicle moving to Carlton Colville. In 1981 a British Trolleybus Society member purchased number 203, moved it to the Oxford Bus Museum for restoration, and then in 1993 moved it to the Sandtoft Trolleybus Museum.

The vehicle's perambulations had not finished, however, and it is seen taking a break between operating turns at the Black Country Museum at Dudley, Worcestershire. Totally dependent on the overhead power supply – other than by its own batteries for 'shunting' purposes – it occasionally makes a visit to bus rallies having been towed by a suitably powerful lorry.

CHASSIS	AEC REGENT V	1963
BODY	EAST LANCS	1963
TYPE	63-SEAT REAR ENTRANCE	

Motor buses were introduced to Cardiff in 1920 and a mixed variety of vehicles has been operated from that time. In line with many municipalities which supported the local economy by placing orders with local companies, part of the Transport Department's policy was to support suppliers who had connections with the city. These included Hall Lewis, Northern Counties, and Air Despatch which became Bruce Coachworks in September 1947. When Bruce was no longer able to supply bodies at the end of 1951 Cardiff continued to order its requirements from East Lancashire Coachbuilders of Blackburn which had supplied the framework to both Air Despatch and Bruce.

The last 27ft-long AEC Regent V model 2D3RA motor buses purchased by the Corporation were bodied by East Lancs with open platform 63-seat highbridge bodywork and arrived in 1963.

Number 408, the example shown, was sold after withdrawal in June 1979 to Way, a dealer in Cardiff who in turn sold it to one of the Barnsley scrapmen. However, before it was collected it was purchased by the Cardiff Regent V Group for preservation. They have restored it back to 1963 condition and from April 1994 it has been loaned by the group to ABACUS, Cardiff which trades as Leisurelink and uses the vehicle on heritage tours in Cardiff. This aspect of preservation, where vehicles are returned to use on what is usually desribed as 'heritage work', is a particularly pleasing development for owners and passengers alike.

The vehicle is seen at the Bristol rally in 1995 promoting its new role with the lettering for the special tours of the Welsh Capital city added to the somewhat sombre Cardiff livery.

SWC 24K

CHASSIS	BRISTOL RE	1972
BODY	ECW	1972
TYPE	53-SEAT FRONT ENTRANCE	

As with private motor cars so some bus designs become classics. Eastern Coach Works built bodies for the Tilling Group and accordingly its products became familiar in many parts of England, Scotland and Wales. Indeed many of its designs could be described at different times as representing 'the typical British Bus'. The ECW design on the Bristol RE chassis, itself a classic, became extremely popular. It was a development of the earlier design seen on page 44 and the improvement in frontal appearance compared to that vehicle, following the introduction of curved windcreen glasses, will be immediately apparent.

In 1928 Colchester Corporation started replacing its small tramway system and 18 trams with motor buses, the last tram running on 8th December 1929. The original buses were Dennis 20-seaters which were followed by other single and double-deck buses of the same make in 1929-30. The first of many AECs arrived in 1930. During the Second World War the venerable Dennis vehicles were replaced by a variety of utility buses allocated between 1942 and 1945.

The first rear-engined buses arrived in 1967-68, being ten Massey-bodied Leyland Atlanteans. Needing to make economies in operating costs – like most other municipalities – Colchester ordered fifteen Bristol RELL6L 36ft-long ECW-bodied single-deck buses seating 53 passengers and one-man-operated. Whilst waiting for these to arrive Colchester purchased six second-hand AEC Reliance single-deckers from SELNEC, these having being built in 1962 and originally supplied to Salford City Transport.

One of the Bristols, number 24, SWC 24K, has survived. New in May 1972 it carries the elegant curved windscreen ECW body which became a standard throughout the country. Withdrawn by Colchester in 1987 it was sold to Lister (PVS) the Bolton dealer who in July of that year sold it for further service to G&G, a Leamington Spa operator. After finishing its original working life in September 1990 it was sold to Guy Stanbury who kept it at the Midland Bus Museum, Wythall as a preserved vehicle. It is seen leaving the Gloucestershire and Warwickshire Railway's station at Toddington, in the Cotswolds, after a rally in June 1994. In November 1995 the vehicle was resold to David Crowther from Booker who plans to return it to PCV service for use on the Heritage Services he operates under contract to Berkshire County Council.

Those wishing to preserve trolleybuses, a mode of transport now unfamiliar with many younger British enthusiasts, have a doubly difficult task ahead of them. Not only do they have to restore the body and running units but they have the added complication of needing a power supply to operate their vehicles. Only a handful of museums have these special facilities and of these Sandtoft, near Doncaster, is one. Power is available at some 500 volts dc through the twin overhead wires, positive and negative, to be collected from the trolleybuses' twin trolley booms – unlike trams where the negative or return to the sub-station is through the steel running rail and thus only one wire is provided.

The metal cowl covering the headlamp, seen right, was designed to reduce the amount of light emitted from vehicles during the wartime blackout in the days when marauding enemy aircraft could be flying low enough to see normal headlights as a means of locating their targets. Trolleybuses and trams introduced a further problem with flashing from the overhead wires and special precautions had to be taken at junctions and termini. The view above shows the use of white paint to make the vehicle somewhat more easy to see in the blackout. The use of the word 'easy' is relative, of course, when virtually nothing could be seen at times.

Derby Corporation introduced trolleybuses in January 1932 and continued to expand the system until April 1958 when the last extension opened to give a maximum system of just 28 route miles. During the war Derby was allocated fifteen Ministry of War Transport utility trolleybuses which had utility bodies built by Park Royal and Weymann on Sunbeam W4 chassis. The harsh outline of the utility body can be seen, with minimal opening windows, and curved domes eliminated to avoid the need for skilled panel beating – before the days of fibreglass mouldings of course. All wartime bodywork had to be built to comply with the utility specification which also included the provision of wooden slatted seats in place of the normal upholstered variety. A utility motor bus body can be seen overleaf.

One of the Weymann-bodied vehicles, No. 172, RC 8472, new in August 1944, was purchased in March 1965 by Michael Dare, who had founded the Reading Transport Society in April 1961.

In 1967 he purchased a former Methodist chapel in Belton on the Isle of Axholme and moved No. 172 there for dry storage.

This chapel became the private Westgate Trolleybus Museum. In 1968 Mr Dare and his mother Mrs D. H. Dare were instrumental in obtaining planning consent for a working trolleybus museum at Sandtoft, a former RAF station a few miles west of Belton and some twelve miles north east of Doncaster.

In November 1969 the first trolleybus arrived on site and at the Sandtoft gathering in September 1972 the first trolleybus to operate from the newly-erected overhead ran in service. At the Sandtoft gathering in July 1995 No. 172 was operating in service, amongst other examples of this almost-forgotten mode of transport, providing excellent photographic opportunities.

DRC 224

CHASSIS	SUNBEAM F4	1952
BODY	WILLOWBROOK	1952
TYPE	60-SEAT REAR ENTRANCE	

Another Derby trolleybus to survive into preservation is this Sunbeam with Willowbrook bodywork. One of 20 delivered to Derby in 1952 it was fitted with BTH electrical equipment. Like the wartime vehicle, seen opposite, it carries the traditional Derby olive green livery which was replaced from May 1969 by the blue and grey paint scheme.

After being withdrawn in 1967, when the trolleybus system closed, number 224 went to the Plumtree Transport Museum in Nottingham. It changed hands and moved to Sandtoft in 1970. After passing through various hands it was sold to the London Trolleybus Preservation Society, its current owner, in 1994 and was moved to Carlton Colville for display at the East Anglian Transport Museum. It was subsequently moved to the Black Country Museum, at Dudley, where this photograph was taken.

SVS 281

CHASSIS	DAIMLER CWA6	1945
BODY	DUPLE UTILITY	1945
TYPE	56-SEAT REAR ENTRANCE	

Passenger vehicle manufacture ceased in 1942 to allow resources to be concentrated on production for the war effort. Because of this curtailment of motor bus chassis manufacture many operators were unable to provide sufficient buses to move the people involved with war work.

Eventually, after some months, the Ministry of War Transport arranged for two manufacturers, Guy Motors Ltd and Transport Vehicles (Daimler) Ltd to produce heavyweight chassis. Most of the Daimler utility buses were fitted with AEC 7.7-litre engines.

Bodywork, from only a handful of designated bodybuilders, was to a strict Utility specification as mentioned overleaf and eliminated unnecessary 'frills' to assist production by semi-skilled labour. Materials needed for the war effort, including aluminium, rubber and good quality hard woods, were eliminated or reduced to the minimum. Opening windows were reduced in number to one pedeck on each side of the vehicle. Later in the war, as supplies eased, a 'Relaxed Utility Specification' was introduced.

The Isle of Man might have seemed an unlikely choice for the allocation of such wartime buses but Douglas Corporation was allocated three Daimler double-deckers during the Second World War to help cater for the extra traffic to and from the Isle of Man Steam Packet Company's boats which sailed from Douglas. The island had a large RAF station at Jurby and many people were held in internment camps for the duration of the war, adding greatly to the need for transport in the island's principal town.

One of the Douglas examples, No. 52, FMN 955, new in 1945 with Duple 56-seat highbridge utility bodywork, was withdrawn from service in March 1970. In July 1970 it was sold to G. Rhodes of Birkenshaw, who had to re-register it as FWW 188J to comply with then current UK legislation. By 1977 it had been bought by Michael Dare and since October 1978 he has kept it at his private Westgate Trolleybus Museum on Humberside.

In May 1993 the Daimler was again re-registered, with a non-dated registration, this time SVS 281. The bright Douglas livery is in contrast to many Utility vehicles which often operated for a good while in drab wartime grey before materials and manpower became available to allow a return to peacetime standards.

Edinburgh Corporation Transport did not operate transport services until 1919 when it exercised its rights to take over the Edinburgh and District Tramway Co. when its lease expired. The 1920 local government reforms merged Leith with Edinburgh and a major reconstruction of the tramways then took place. Edinburgh converted the cable tramway systems which it acquired from the Tramway Company to conventional electric traction with overhead supply, compatible with the Leith system which had been electrified in 1905.

The first motor buses were introduced on 29th December 1919 when a number of Leyland normal-control buses were put on a regular route between Ardmillan Terrace and Abbeyhill.

Leyland and AEC buses predominated until the first Daimler's arrival in 1929; two Morris-Commercial Imperials arrived in 1933. Between 1935 and 1939 when a policy of using double-deck buses wherever possible was introduced, 51 Daimler COG6 were purchased with a further 65 Daimler single-deck buses of model COG5/40 for use on routes with low bridges.

Various types of utility vehicles arrived during the war whilst the first peacetime arrivals included AEC, Bristol, Crossley and Guy as well as the favoured Daimler.

To replace the trams a fleet of 321 Leyland PD2s, 70 Guy Arab IV and 60 second-hand wartime Guy Arabs from London Transport were placed in service between 1953 and 1956. The London Guys were fitted with new bodies by Duple before being placed into service and one of these (not shown) has survived into preservation.

OFS 777		
CHASSIS	**LEYLAND PD2/20**	**1957**
BODY	**MCW**	**1957**
TYPE	**63-SEAT REAR ENTRANCE**	

Edinburgh's last tram ran on 16th November 1956 before the last of the new buses mentioned above had arrived. Fleet No. 777, OFS 777, part of the replacement fleet, was placed in service in January 1957 and was one of the last batch of 40 Leyland Titan PD2/20 with Metro-Cammell H34/29R rear open platform double-deck bodies to be bought by Edinburgh. Local supplier Alexander bodied all subsequent double-deck buses for the city until 1981.

The Orion body seen here was built at a time when an ultra lightweight specification was in vogue to reduce weight and, supposedly, cut running costs. Although Edinburgh insisted on having some opening windows included in the design it was a far cry from the Scottish city's normal standard – 'masses of shivering tin' was an apt description of the buses from one Baillie, and his word-picture has passed into transport folklore.

In May 1974 it was withdrawn from service and transferred to the training fleet being renumbered T9. After Lothian Regional Transport took over Edinburgh in May 1975, it was renumbered TB9 in 1976. In June 1982 it was sold for preservation to Jamieson and Partners who sold it to Kelvin Scottish in March 1986 for use as a driver trainer.

The attraction for this major operator was the vehicle's synchromesh gearbox which allowed drivers to be trained on a manual transmission bus. All Kelvin's vehicles by this time had either semi- or fully-automatic transmission and drivers could only obtain a licence for the type of vehicle on which they had been trained. Clearly this could be restrictive. Whilst with Kelvin Scottish the bus carried fleet number L326, then 1997 and finally 0997.

In April 1991 it was again sold for preservation, this time being acquired by the Lothian Bus Club, Edinburgh who since September 1995 have kept it at the Scottish Vintage Bus Museum at Lathalmond near Dumfermline. Let us hope that its days of frequent moves and never-ending number changes have finished.

CORSTORPHINE

ENTER BY
REAR
ENTRANCE

YSG 101

YSG 101

CHASSIS	LEYLAND LEOPARD PSU3/1R	1961
BODY	ALEXANDER	1961
TYPE	33-SEAT TRIPLE DOOR	

In April 1961 Mr W. M. Little, Edinburgh's Transport Manager, arranged for an export Leyland Olympic 35ft-long single-deck bus intended for Cuba to be inspected in Edinburgh by his Transport Committee. Mr Little was still unable to operate double-deck buses on some routes due to low bridges and realised that if large capacity single-deck buses built to dimensions used on the continent and elsewhere could be legalised for use in Britain, he could replace some double-deck buses with large capacity standee vehicles.

In August 1961 the legislation was indeed altered to allow 36ft-long buses and coaches to be used in Britain and Edinburgh quickly ordered a Leyland PSU3/1R chassis, to be fitted with a special Alexander 35-seat body with three entrance/exits. This vehicle, No. 101, was displayed at the 1961 Scottish Motor Show in Glasgow before returning to Leyland Motors for modification and testing. By the time it returned to Edinburgh in late December its seating capacity had been reduced to 33 and it could carry 40 standees, passengers entering by the rear door and passing the seated conductor. In early 1962 it was again returned to Leyland, this time for demonstration to the Ulster Transport in Northern Ireland for trials to see if a 36ft-long vehicle could be used there. After those trials the Ulster Government changed the necessary legislation to allow such vehicles to operate in Northern Ireland.

During March 1962 number 101 was used for crew training before entering service on the 16 route, Comiston to Silverknowes, on Sunday 29th April. It is believed to be the first stage service bus built to these new dimensions to have entered service in Britain.

After local Government reorganisation in Scotland in May 1975 No. 101 passed into the Lothian Regional Transport fleet and was withdrawn and sold in May 1988 to D. Scoular, an Edinburgh enthusiast, for preservation. The vehicle had been out of use since before 1985.

It is seen in pristine condition parked at the Gateshead Metro Centre in 1995, only minutes before a torrential hailstorm washed out the transport event. It is an example of the standee concept with its 'new-fangled three-door layout' which did not gain favour in Edinburgh, nor indeed in Britain as a whole.

ASC 690B

CHASSIS	LEYLAND PD3/6	1964
BODY	ALEXANDER	1964
TYPE	70-SEAT FORWARD ENTRANCE	

A distinctive feature of Edinburgh's buses has always been their distinctive and very impressive livery. The rich madder red, with contrasting white relief, including the whole of the roof and discreet gold lining was always attractive and, more importantly, always well kept. It is an object lesson in how a fleet can be kept immaculate if there is a will.

Edinburgh received its first forward-entrance 30ft-long double-deck buses in 1964, when 50 Leyland PD3/6 examples arrived carrying Alexander 70-seat bodywork. Increasing use of fibreglass resin for domes and smaller components was commonplace by this time but Alexander's design team pressed ahead on a more ambitious level. Eventually large sub-assemblies were moulded in what became known as grp (glass reinforced plastic) and a complete staircase unit was produced at the Falkirk works for inclusion in the company's bodywork.

Number 690, ASC 690B, was placed in service in September and remained until July 1977 when Lothian Regional Transport withdrew it and sold it to Locke, an Edinburgh dealer, who resold it for non PSV use to Baird of Auchterhouse who used it seasonally until 1990 when it was purchased for preservation by J. Mason from Edinburgh.

It is seen at the Gateshead Metro Centre during a rally there in 1995. The space available is put to good use at this event and photographers and visitors alike can see the vehicles more easily since they are not crammed together as is the case at so many rallies.

During that same year Scottish bus preservation took a great leap forward with the acquisition of land at Lathalmond, near Dunfermline, where an ambitious museum is being created. Forty-two acres allow space enough to house vehicles in buildings set aside for different operators, whilst providing ample space for restoration and renovation. A vintage bus service will operate around the site, off public roads.

KHC 369

CHASSIS	AEC REGENT V	**1963**
BODY	EAST LANCS	**1963**
TYPE	60-SEAT REAR ENTRANCE	

Eastbourne Corporation claims to be the first municipality in the world to have started running motor bus services though in fact that honour rightly belongs to Southampton. In April 1903 Eastbourne hired a 14-seat Milnes-Daimler single-deck bus for ten days to work an experimental service between the railway station and Meads and, encouraged by the receipts taken the trial bus, three others were purchased. In 1904 after trials involving two Clarkson steam buses which did not stay long. Milnes-Daimlers remained the favourite until 1907 when four De Dion open-top double-deckers were purchased. In 1912 the first Leyland arrived. Leyland became the favourite make until 1933 when only six of the 55 petrol-engined buses in the Corporation's fleet were not Leylands. The first diesel-engined bus arrived in 1946. The post-war fleet included AEC, Crossley, and Leyland double-deck buses and one AEC Regal single-deck bus.

The last four AEC Regent V model 2D3RV double-deck motor buses for this fleet arrived in 1963 and like most of Eastbourne's post-war buses were fitted with bodies built by East Lancs, this time with seating for 60 passengers, and translucent roof panels in the upper saloon. Two of the four were fitted with platform doors.

One of these, No. 69, new in May 1963, was withdrawn in December 1980 by Eastbourne Borough Transport which, after local Government changes in April 1974, had taken over the Corporation's activities. It was purchased by R. Thrower and colleagues for preservation. In December 1988 ownership was transferred to the 69 Fund.

In February 1993 it was sold, this time to A. Beadnall of Saltburn, who kept it until December 1993 when Brian Birks, from Abingdon, acquired it. Its last change of owner was in September 1994 when Ken Hulks of Doncaster became its proud owner.

The photograph shows the vehicle operating a park-and-ride service at the Sandtoft Trolleybus Museum in 1995. Another member of the batch, number 67, an example without rear platform doors, is also preserved and appears regularly at various rallies. It was another of the visitors to the Nottingham AEC Rally in May 1995.

GEX 740F

CHASSIS	LEYLAND ATLANTEAN	1964
BODY	MCW	1964
TYPE	70-SEAT FRONT ENTRANCE	

Great Yarmouth Corporation Tramways opened on 19th June, 1902 and was unusual in that the Corporation operated two unconnected systems. The main one used 23 trams in the principal section, north of the river Yare. The other used 12 trams linking Southtown and Gorleston.

In 1920 three second-hand motor buses were purchased from the London General Omnibus Company. They were AEC 'B'-type open-top double-deckers seating 34 passengers. When these became unservicable at the end of the 1924 season, three more identical buses were bought from LGOC, these running seasonally until the end of 1927.

When tramway abandonment started a fleet of seven Guy model BB single-deck buses replaced the first route on 15th May 1924. These were fitted with 30 seat dual-entrance bodies built by United Automobile Services Ltd in nearby Lowestoft whose body-building activities passed to Eastern Coach Works Ltd in the 1930s. In 1927 and 1928 four similar buses arrived with pneumatic tyres and in 1928 five Guy model FCX six-wheel forward-control double-deck buses with Short Bros (Rochester) Ltd 56-seat bodies arrived to be followed by ten Guy single-deck buses fitted with Guy bodies in 1929 and 1930. In 1931 the first AEC Regent double-deck buses arrived with United bodies, the last tram running on 14th December 1933. Since then Leyland, AEC and Guy buses have been bought

Great Yarmouth was the first operator to introduce a one-man operated double-deck bus when this became possible on 1st July 1966, and a Leyland Atlantean double-deck bus with Roe body was used with both decks open to passengers. With standardisation in mind three single-deck Leyland Atlantean PDR1/2 buses were delivered in 1968, with bodies built by Marshall, the Cambridge bodybuilder, as fleet numbers 40-42. Only two municipalities purchased Atlanteans for use as single-deck buses. Number 40, new in 1968, was loaned to the Great Yarmouth Atlantean Group after withdrawal in April 1983. The group changed its name in May 1984 to the Anglian PSV Preservation Society.

By May 1987 number 40 had been bought by the PK Historic Omnibus Co, Hunmanby. In August 1988 it was purchased by J. Sykes, a dealer of Carlton, Barnsley who sold it the same month to P. Hilton of Blackpool. In April 1989 it was acquired by Jim Stones of Glazebury for use as a PSV. By late 1990 it was for sale again. This time R. Davis from Douglas, Isle of Man, purchased it in May 1991 and the bus is now kept at the St. Helens Museum of Transport.

It is seen in a particularly attractive corner of the car park at the Heart of the Pennines, Halifax, event in May 1994, marking the start of another successful event for Tony Blackman and his supporters.

BCP 671

CHASSIS	AEC REGENT III	1950
BODY	PARK ROYAL	1950
TYPE	56-SEAT REAR ENTRANCE	

The distinctive Halifax livery seen here has often aroused speculation as to its similarity with the Glasgow colour scheme.

Halifax Corporation commenced operating electric tramway services on 29th December 1898. On 17th October 1912 it started its first motor bus route using Daimler CC single-deck buses, the livery for both trams and buses being maroon.

After the railway companies obtained powers to operate motor bus services in 1928 to protect their interests from increasing competition from road transport, Halifax entered into an agreement, effective from 1st April 1929, to co-ordinate bus services in the Halifax area. Halifax Corporation continued to operate bus services within the borough, the 'A' fleet. In a specified area outside the borough a 'B' fleet was operated by Halifax Corporation on behalf of the Joint Omnibus Committee which was owned by the Corporation with a half share, the LMS railway with a third share, the remaining one-sixth being owned by the LNE railway.

During early 1929 the Corporation had placed orders for three single-deck buses for evaluation and at the same time three AEC Regent double-deck buses were ordered with Short Bros bodies. The three AECs were painted in a new livery introduced by the Corporation and JOC to distinguish its vehicles from other operators in the area. Also at this time MT 2114, the prototype AEC Regent, was painted in the same colour scheme of orange, green and cream being very similar to the livery introduced in 1928 for Glasgow Corporation double-deck buses but lacking Glasgow's grey roofs. Halifax buses were painted with a green roof.

When G. F. Craven, a director of Park Royal Coachworks, resigned to become the manager at Halifax in late 1933 it was perhaps not surprising that Park Royal became the most favoured supplier of bodies for its AECs, Roe being its regular alternate supplier.

'B' fleet No. 277, BCP 671, is typical of the 58 7ft 6in-wide AEC Regent III type 9612E model buses purchased in the early post-war years with Park Royal 56-seat bodies for both the 'A' and 'B' fleets. A further sixteen with 8ft-wide bodies went to the 'B' fleet for use on routes where the traffic commissioners between 1946 and 1950 exercised their discretion. Note the unusually slim body pillars – the design was derived from PRV's Utility body structure.

Number 277 was renumbered 377 between 1959 and September 1967 when it was restored by the Halifax manager, Mr Geoffrey Hilditch, as No. 277. In May 1969 it was sold to A. R. Blackman for continued preservation. Tony has continued to rally the vehicle and in 1995 No. 277 was recertified for service as a PCV and is now available for that 'special occasion'. It is seen leaving the Halifax Piece Hall at the Heart of the Pennines bus rally which in 1995 commemorated the 50th anniversary of VE day.

GJX 331

CHASSIS	DAIMLER CVG6	1956
BODY	ROE	1956
TYPE	65-SEAT REAR ENTRANCE	

In November 1956 the Halifax Corporation 'A' fleet (see previous page) took delivery of five Daimler CVG6 motor buses, fleet Nos. 15 to 19, GJX 327-331, which were fitted with Roe 65-seat bodies. In an effort to make fuel economies the weight of the traditional Roe body was reduced by constructing the upper deck using an aluminium frame instead of the more usual teak frame.

In July 1958 these vehicles were renumbered 115 to 119 and then in January 1971 they were transferred to the JOC 'B' fleet as Nos. 300-304. In September 1971 the 'B' fleet came under the ownership of Calderdale JOC when the 'B' fleet at Halifax merged with Todmorden JOC. The railway interests in both fleets came under the control of APT (Amalgamated Passenger Transport Co Ltd). In July 1972 No. 304 was renumbered 384 before being withdrawn from service in 1973.

Number 384 survived, however, to be transferred to the West Yorkshire PTE in April 1974 being stored by the PTE at Bramley until in March 1981 it was sold for preservation to N. Whiteley of Queensbury. During 1982 it was stored at the premises of the former Tameside Transport Collection in the one-time municipal transport depot at Ashton-under-Lyne.

In November 1984 the vehicle was sold to the West Yorkshire Transport Museum at Bradford which, over a period of time, restored it as Halifax 'A' fleet No. 119. It is now fully restored for passenger use at 'Transperience', The West Yorkshire Transport Discovery Park, Low Moor, Bradford which opened in July 1995.

It is seen here at the rally held at the Metro Centre, Gateshead on 14th May 1995 which was organised by the Go Ahead Northern Bus Enthusiasts Association.

The instant giveaway for a Roe body built to the traditional teak-framed design, the raised waistrail beneath the lower deck windows, is clearly visible. Note also the plain black fleet numerals on the front of this vehicle and 35, opposite, contrasting with the outline rear numerals.

PJX 35

CHASSIS	LEYLAND LEOPARD L1	1962
BODY	WEYMANN	1962
TYPE	42-SEAT FRONT ENTRANCE	

The introduction of the under-floor engined single-decker bus has been mentioned on page 15 with the Bournemouth vehicle. Each manufacturer had its own models and Leyland followed the heavyweight Royal Tiger with the equally famous lighter weight Tiger Cub .

The Leyland 'Leopard' was introduced in 1959 to meet the needs of operators who had found the 'Tiger Cub' to be underpowered and Leyland fitted the larger O.600 engine to what was a basically a Tiger Cub chassis. It remained in production from 1959 in various forms until 1983 being replaced by the later Leyland 'Tiger' introduced in 1981.

In 1962 Halifax purchased sixteen Leyland Leopard model L1 single-deck buses with 42-seat Weymann bodies. The Corporation 'A' fleet took nine as fleet Nos. 31-39 and the JOC 'B' fleet had the other seven as fleet Nos. 232-238. They were all still in service when the West Yorkshire PTE was formed in 1974, No. 35, the preserved example, becoming WYPTE 3035. In February 1981 No. 3035 was sold to Dave Sayer from Halifax for preservation.

After restoration it was then sold to the West Yorkshire Transport Museum which had also acquired similar No. 232. In December 1990 Dave Sayer repurchased No. 35 and further restoration work was carried out. In its 19 years of service it had covered over 750,000 miles in the arduous Halifax terrain.

The Weymann body was another classic of its time, being seen in many BET fleets as well as with municipalities and independent operators. The large front indicators change the appearance quite substantially but the rear is absolutely typical of the neat well planned design which could be seen on a variety of chassis.

The Leopard badge on the front was one of a series to a basically similar design which had originated with the Royal Tiger, and included amongst others the Panther and Atlantean. Note the single spot lamp, legal at that time, whilst the rear view shows the obligatory emergency exit required by law on a bus fitted with a front entrance/exit.

192 OTB

CHASSIS	LEYLAND TITAN PD2/41	1960
BODY	EAST LANCS	1960
TYPE	59-SEAT REAR ENTRANCE	

Haslingden Corporation was unusual in that when it purchased the portion of a steam tramway within its boundaries on 1st January 1908 it only worked it until 4th September 1908, when electric tramcars belonging to Accrington Corporation started operating through Haslingden to the Rawtenstall boundary at Lockgate.

Haslingden introduced its first motor bus on 12th November 1907 with a Leyland 'X' type single-deck bus which ran intermittently until early 1911.

After the First World War buses reappeared with the introduction of a variety of types made by BSA, Austin, Guy and Leyland when an express bus service, in which Haslingden participated with the other two operators, started between Accrington and Rawtenstall on 3rd December 1928.

Three utility buses, two Daimlers and one Guy joined the fleet during the Second World War. These were followed by a variety of Leylands until 1968 when, after Haslingden and Rawtenstall had shared the same manager for a number of years, a Rossendale Joint Transport Committee was formed to combine the two bus fleets. The attractive blue and cream livery on the 17 Haslingden buses was replaced by the Rawtenstall maroon and cream. In 1974 local government reorganisation created a new Borough of Rossendale with the Joint Committee ceasing to exist, becoming instead the Transport Department of the new council.

Vehicle No. 192 OTB is a Leyland Titan PD2/41 motor bus supplied to Haslingden Corporation in 1960 as fleet No. 14. Local bodybuilder East Lancs built the attractive 59-seat body. It was renumbered 44 in the joint fleet and survived in service until 1978. After being used as a driver trainer, it was stored until March 1992 when it was sold for preservation to G. Goldthorpe of Batley. In February 1993 Chris Nadin from York purchased it, in turn selling it to S. M. Torres, also from York, for preservation. It is now restored in its Haslingden livery as No. 14, is a reminder of one of Lancashire's smallest municipalities, and joins other unusual and interesting buses owned by Mr Torres which regularly visit the rallies.

JVH 373

CHASSIS	AEC REGENT III	1955
BODY	EAST LANCS L/BRIDGE	1955
TYPE	58-SEAT REAR ENTRANCE	

Huddersfield is unique amongst British municipalities in being the first to operate its own transport department.

The terms of the 1870 Tramways Act specifically precluded local authority operation but such was the nature of the hilly Huddersfield terrain that when the tramways had been built no commercial operator was prepared to take on the lease to operate the system. The Corporation thus had to obtain Parliamentary powers to allow it to operate the system.

Steam trams started operating on 11th January 1883, and on 14th February 1901 the first electric trams started to run. Tramcar operation ceased on 29th June 1940.

Motor bus services commenced on 20th December 1920, and by March 1929 its fleet of 64 buses was completely of one make, all being built in Huddersfield by Karrier Motors Ltd. Two Guys and two Brockways had been withdrawn earlier.

On 16th May 1930 the Corporation entered into an agreement with the LMS Railway for all bus services to be operated by the Huddersfield Joint Omnibus Committee and unlike the other railway agreements there was only a 'B' fleet, with the Corporation and the LMSR being equal partners. When the trams were replaced between 1933 and 1940 the Corporation was able to operate trackless trolley vehicles without prejudicing the agreement since, legally, these were not buses.

During the Second World War Huddersfield was allocated nineteen Daimler utility lowbridge type motor buses which allowed certain Holme Valley services which had been operated by highbridge buses to be replaced with lowbridge vehicles. These did not need to be in the centre of the road when passing under the bridge on Woodhead Road, Lockwood, a practice which was highly dangerous in the wartime blackout or in foggy weather when in both cases the driver's vision was restricted.

Post-war purchases continued to include lowbridge buses for these services, but on AEC chassis. The last three examples were delivered in 1955, and the last of these, No. 243, on a 9613 chassis fitted with an East Lancs 58-seat lowbridge body, has survived into preservation.

Like all the odd-numbered vehicles in the fleet it was owned by the railway half of the JOC. Even-numbered vehicles belonged to the Corporation.

After withdrawal in 1973 it was purchased for preservation by Brian Goulding from Poulton-le-Fylde, later to be the founder of the AEC Society. Its next two owners came from Halifax and during this time the vehicle was stored at various sites used by members of the Mersey and Calder Bus Preservation Group.

After moving to Meltham No. 243 was purchased by E. Glyn Sykes of Huddersfield, who now keeps it at the MCBPG premises at Meltham Mills. Glyn, a former Hanson bus driver on the Meltham route, has spent considerable time and money in restoring Huddersfield's last lowbridge bus.

It is used on many of the free bus services which Tony Blackman organises at Halifax and Meltham.

HUM 401

CHASSIS	AEC REGENT	1940
BODY	ROE	1940
TYPE	56-SEAT REAR ENTRANCE	

Leeds changed the colour of its vehicles several times during the undertaking's existence – yellow giving way to blue and then green, whilst the trams went from blue to crimson. The pre-war blue livery survives on at least three preserved Leeds vehicles, one of which is shown here.

Leeds Corporation operated trams between February 1894 and 7th November 1959. On 20th June 1911 it started to operate trolleybuses to Farnley as a feeder route to the trams. Eventually Leeds trolleybuses operated from Guiseley to Otley and Burley, before being withdrawn from 26th July 1928.

The Corporation started operating motor buses on 30th October 1913, and developed an extensive system. It was another of the Yorkshire municipalities which operated buses jointly with the railway companies. The agreement became effective from April 1929, with 23 buses in the Leeds 'B' fleet being jointly owned. It was terminated in July 1931 when Leeds refused to surrender tram routes in the joint 'B' fleet area, if or when tramway conversion might cause their abandonment.

The early motor buses used by Leeds included Daimler open-top double-deckers. During the 1920s Crossley, Guy, Karrier, Dennis and Halley vehicles were used with most of the bodies being built in Leeds by C. H. Roe at its Cross Gates Carriage Works.

During the 1930s the chassis orders were mainly AEC with some Leyland and a few Crossley Condor and Dennis Lances in 1930-32. It became the practice for a Leeds motor bus with a Roe body to appear at the Commercial Motor Show, examples being number 200 in 1935 – a full-fronted AEC – and number 400, another AEC Regent, in 1937.

Among the last buses to typical late pre-war pattern was No. 106, HUM 401. An AEC Regent, it was new in 1940 and fitted with 7.7-litre engine, preselective gearbox and a 56-seat Roe body, as seen here.

Withdrawn in November 1956 it was used as a driver trainer bus until March 1962, subsequently being used as a decorated bus later that year. It had become a mobile office by 1967 and was still owned by Leeds Corporation when the West Yorkshire PTE was formed in April 1974.

The PTE restored the bus, and it was repainted into the pre-war Leeds livery of pale blue with cream relief and a grey roof. It was then used for promotional purposes.

In October 1986 ownership passed to Yorkshire Rider, the vehicle being classed as a non-PSV. It was allocated number H309 for accountancy purposes, but is preserved in original Leeds condition.

Three-axle double-decker buses were rare outside London and this fine Leicester example shows a type extant in the 'thirties.

Leicester City Transport acquired the horse trams and buses of the Leicester Tramway Company on 1st January 1901 and commenced to convert the system to electric traction, which was introduced in May 1904 when the first 60 trams were placed in service.

Motor buses did not appear until 1924 when six single-deck Tilling Stevens TS6 petrol electric buses were placed in service in July. After a further seven double-deck TS6 arrived in 1925, Leicester purchased a variety of Guy single-deck and double-deck buses, the latter being normal-control three-axle examples. During the 1930s various AEC Regents, Leyland Titans and a Crossley Condor were purchased.

When the question of tramway replacement became pertinent in the late 1930s consideration was given to replacing the tramcars with trolleybuses because of their larger carrying capability. A compromise solution was the purchase of large capacity double-deck motor buses with 66 seats (nearly as big as the trams) instead. The model chosen was the three-axle AEC Renown with 7.7-litre engine and preselective gearbox. Northern Counties and Metro-Cammell-built the bodies, and 25 entered service between February 1939 and June 1940.

In 1957-58 they were withdrawn from service and No. 329, CBC 921, was purchased in May 1958 by members of the Vintage Passenger Vehicle Society, ownership passing to the Historic Commercial Vehicle Club in 1962.

The HCVC placed the vehicle on display at the Measham Motor Museum in the mid-1960s and then, when space was available, it was moved to Carlton Colville until it was placed on permanent loan by the HCVC in March 1973, to the Leicestershire Museum of Technology. Museum staff have since restored the bus to its original splendid appearance and condition and the finished restoration is seen at the AEC Rally held at Nottingham in May 1994.

The bulbous front domes are typical of NCME bodies of the time whilst the large and very clear destination display, particularly the route numbers, is typical of Leicester practice.

DFE 383

CHASSIS	GUY ARAB III	1948
BODY	GUY (PRV FRAMED)	1948
TYPE	56-SEAT REAR ENTRANCE	

This vehicle has much in common with Southampton No. 71 seen on page 66, yet differs in two important aspects. The familiar Guy radiator has been replaced by a rather inelegant substitute, and the body is actually a Guy product.

Lincoln City Transport acquired the horse tram route of the Lincoln Tramway Co Ltd in 1904, the Corporation substituting electric trams on 3rd November 1905. Motor buses were introduced in 1920 and by 1927 some 27 single-deck Dennis and Guy buses had been purchased.

In December 1927 the Corporation was the purchaser of the first production Leyland TD1, lowheight double-deck bus, after Leyland demonstrated it could negotiate the Stonebow Arch at the north end of the High Street. This allowed the Corporation to substitute buses on its sole tram route on 3rd March 1929 and use these throughout the city.

A variety of different types of vehicles was purchased during the 'thirties. After receiving Guy Arab double-deck buses during the war, its early purchases after the war included Leylands with Roe bodies in addition to ten Guy Arab III double-deck buses with bodies built by Guy Motors using Park Royal frames. The rear emergency exit door with its raised lower edges was a characteristic Park Royal feature of the time, giving a pointer to the body designer.

Number 23, the first of these, was the first Guy to be fitted with a Meadows 10.35 litre engine and was exhibited at the 1948 Commercial Motor Show prior to delivery to Lincoln, the other nine having conventional Gardner engines. In February 1953 its Meadows engine was replaced by a Leyland 8.6-litre engine removed from a withdrawn vehicle. In 1961 No. 23 was fitted with an experimental Ruston and Hornsby air-cooled engine (see overleaf for further details).

When the bus was withdrawn it was acquired in November 1967 by the Lincolnshire Vintage Vehicle Society and repainted in LVVS livery. In 1983 the LVVS restored the bus to its 1950 style of Lincoln City Transport livery.

It is seen at the Meltham Experience organised by the Mersey & Calder Bus Preservation Group in July 1994.

Almost always, buses in the United Kingdom have used the traditional water-cooled engine but in the 'fifties and 'sixties there was a move to experiment with air cooled engines. Probably the most famous exponent of this method of cooling is the Volkswagen Beetle, and it is perhaps no coincidence that air cooled commercial vehicle engines were also popular in Germany. The lack of a conventional radiator on this vehicle is the immediate clue to the method of cooling involved.

The attraction lay in the elimination of the cooling system with its potential for leaking, freezing, and requirement for expensive anti-freeze additives. There was a distinct disadvantage in that buses so fitted tended to be extremely noisy. Drivers and conductors who worked on this Lincoln vehicle recall that in the lower saloon it was virtually impossible to hear oneself speak and passengers communicated with the conductor through sign language.

The main manufacturer was the German Deutz Company, but Ruston & Hornsby built some experimental engines. The latter used Lincoln, the local operator, as a convenient means of progressing its experiments. Ruston and its predecessors had been pioneers in the development of the internal combustion engine but had not been involved with diesel engines until this period.

Only very few operators tried air-cooled engines in Britain and none continued for long. Some subsequently refitted the original water-cooled units after deciding against the concept. The Lincoln vehicle is thus an unusual survivor of an interesting experiment.

CHASSIS	GUY OTTER LLOD	1954
BODY	ROE	1954
TYPE	25-SEAT FORWARD ENTRANCE	

CCC 596

Llandudno Urban District Council was an unusual motor bus operator. Between 1928 and 1951 it operated seasonal 'Run-About' tours for holidaymakers along the private Marine Drive which encircled the Great Orme headland.

The first two runabouts, a Guy and a Dennis, both had toastrack bodies and in 1929 were joined by four others from Dennis with Roberts toastrack bodies. In the late 1930s two Guy 'Wolf' and one Commer PN3 were purchased. After the war a fleet of Guy Wolf chassis with either Barnard or Metalcraft bodies were acquired, including three handsome forward-control examples.

In 1951 the Llanduno Urban District Council was successful in obtaining a stage carriage licence to operate an all-year service for the benefit of residents who lived on the Orme. This involved climbing up a maximum gradient of 1 in 3.6 and special dispensation was granted allowing the use of a public service vehicle on this route, the steepest bus route in Britain. The first two buses purchased for this route were supplied by Foden, the Sandbach builder of goods vehicles, which had developed a PSV chassis after the war. A modified version of this chassis was used with sprag gears being incorporated in the back axle. These would prevent the vehicle running backwards down the gradient in the event of a transmission failure. In addition, special low ratio gearboxes were fitted.

In 1954 two smaller Guy Otter model LLOD buses, with Gardner 4LK engines, were purchased for use in quieter periods. These had 25-seat bodies built by Roe, with sunshine roofs. Like the Fodens they had to be fitted with special rear axles incorporating sprag gearing.

Vehicle CCC 596 new in April 1954, had in April 1974 become the property of Aberconwy Council, the successor to Llandudno UDC. In November 1982 it was sold to J. Harris of Clayton-le-Woods for preservation. It was used on a bus service linking the textile museum at Helmshore with the East Lancs Railway, Rossendale Transport hiring it in September and October 1987 and again from April to the end of October in 1988. In July 1993 Mr Hughes of Alpine Coaches, Llandudno repurchased it for preservation and to return it to use as a PCV (formerly PSV until 1990) on heritage services.

This Guy single-decker is one of the best-known preserved buses on the rally circuit. JC 5313 has been rallied continuously since August 1967. Over the years it has been overhauled, including major attention to the bodywork, and has had two full repaints since 1962.

Llandudno was unusual in that seven of its pre-war vehicles, and eight from the post-war fleet, survived to be bought for preservation, an unusually high percentage. The majority of the preserved examples were petrol-engined.

By 1960 only 47 of the 17,000 municipal buses then operating in Britain were petrol-engined, the others using diesel fuel. Six double-deckers in Douglas were to become the last such municipal examples in Britain, whilst of the 41 single-deckers most were operating seasonal holiday services at Blackpool, Colwyn Bay, Llandudno, Portsmouth and Southport.

In January 1965 Llandudno UDC sold its last two pre-war buses, JC 4557, a Commer, and JC 5313, this Guy, to D. G. Owen, a local fuel oil distributor, for use as store sheds.

In September 1965 both vehicles were sold to T. G. Cadman of Bognor Regis, for preservation. The Commer was collected and rallied but due to a siezed engine the Guy was still in Mr Owen's yard in September 1966 when enthusiast Geoff Lumb saw it. After two months of negotiations JC 5313 became his property, leaving its new owner with the problem of moving it home to Huddersfield, which was done in January 1967.

After eight months' work the Guy was mobile, and its external appearance was tidied up before it was repainted in original livery. Although this looked correct in wet weather, in sunlight the maroon paint appeared to be too light.

This difficulty in matching colours is one of the side effects following the change in paint composition since new health and safety legislation requires reduced levels of lead in paint. Modern paints lack the body which pre-war paints had, and this is the reason that many fleets changed to lighter shades in the 1950s.

Eastern Coach Works bodies, built in Lowestoft, are normally associated with the big company fleets – Tilling and NBC – but bodies were also built for smaller operators. It was appropriate that ECW should build for the local municipality and happily an example has been preserved, as shown.

Lowestoft Corporation, the easternmost one in Britain, introduced electric trams to the town on 22nd July 1903 on a single cross town route linking Pakefield in the south to the borough boundary on the Yarmouth Road, north of the town. In 1927 motor buses were introduced as feeders to the tram routes.

During early 1931 the northern part of the tram route was replaced with Guy single-deck buses, with eight AEC Regent double-deck buses replacing the trams to Pakefield on 8th May 1931. It was fourteen years before the next new buses arrived in 1945 when five Guy utility double-deck buses were allocated by the Ministry of War Transport.

Lowestoft supported local industry quite commendably so far as its body requirements were concerned. The first five buses in 1927-8 were fitted with bodies built by Waveney at Oulton Broad, and of the 52 buses owned by the Corporation only 16 were not produced by local labour.

The April 1974 local government changes created a larger local authority – Waveney District Council – into which Lowestoft was absorbed. Since the majority of services in this new area were provided by Eastern Counties Omnibus Company Ltd a co-ordination agreement was agreed with ECOC but when this proved unprofitable the new Waveney District Council found itself in a difficult financial situation and tried to regain control of its services in 1975 to take effect from March 1976.

Eastern Counties succeeded in obtaining new operating licences and Waveney was forced into losing those services, then finding that its sole remaining route and school services were financially unable to support the operation. On 3rd December 1977 the Waveney District Council ceased to operate buses and all local services are now provided by Eastern Counties.

The remaining twelve Waveney DC vehicles were sold in 1978 with the newest two vehicles, the 1973 AEC Swifts, being purchased by Great Yarmouth Borough Transport.

The Swift was a rear-engined chassis and this body design was an adaptation of the standard ECW product for the infinitely more successful Bristol RE design which sold in large numbers.

The last of the 1969 AEC Swifts, No. 4, YRT 898H with dual-door ECW body seating 47 and carrying 20 standees, was sold in January 1978 to a Barnsley dealer. By July 1978 it had been bought by operator Fosdike of Bramfield who stored the vehicle, without having used it, until October 1988 when it was moved to the East Anglia Transport Museum at Carlton Colville on the outskirts of Lowestoft.

It has since been restored as Lowestoft No. 4 and is seen here at the May 1995 AEC Rally. Note the flat windscreen glasses as compared to Colchester No. 24 on page 23.

JND 646

DETAILS OVERLEAF

45

Manchester operated one of the largest bus fleets in the country and for many years had vehicles built to its own distinctive style. Even in the late 'thirties it was placing large enough orders – and was prepared to pay the extra cost – to be able to persuade Leyland to modify the standard Bailey body to suit the Corporation's streamlined outline.

Manchester Corporation operated trams from 6th June 1901 and, despite the opposition of manager Stuart Pilcher, trolleybuses were subsequently introduced on some of the routes to the east of the city as tramway replacements. These operated between 1st January 1938 and 30th December 1966 when the last route was abandoned. The last tramcar ran on 10th January 1949.

Motor buses were introduced in 1914 and continued until 31st October 1969 when Manchester became the major contributor with 1,239 vehicles when SELNEC PTE was formed to take over the municipal operators in South East Lancashire and North East Cheshire.

Before the Second War Manchester had favoured Crossley and Leyland chassis but after that war Crossley orders decreased and the favoured makes were Leyland and Daimler, with only very limited numbers of other makes being purchased.

The Corporation's livery was vermillion and off white, as seen in these photographs, except for vehicles painted blue for use on airport and, later, other selected services.

JND 646

CHASSIS	LEYLAND TITAN PD2/3	1951
BODY	METRO CAMMELL	1951
TYPE	58-SEAT REAR ENTRANCE	

This Leyland Titan carries the standard post-war Manchester style of body, in this case manufactured by Metro Cammell but also supplied to the Corporation by Crossley and Brush.

Number 3245, a Leyland PD2/3, was new in November 1951 and fitted with a 58-seat body built to the Corporation's post-war design where the rear platform structure is suspended from the bodywork instead of being supported by an extension to the chassis frame.

The reason for designing the body in this manner was to reduce potential damage to the rear chassis members when a bus suffered a rear end collision. It reflects the then normal practice of routinely separating bodies from chassis at overhaul, or to repair serious damage.

The additional body framing for the cantilever construction resulted in the last two downstairs windows in the lower saloon being shallower than the others, the last two bays in the upper saloon having shallow windows for the same reason. Crossley also sold bodies of this design to other operators, as seen on page 13.

Number 3245 was in the Manchester fleet when SELNEC took over in November 1969 and was not withdrawn until March 1971. It was then purchased by E. Gibbons and R. MacMullen.

In May 1973 it passed to the SELNEC Transport Society, which was renamed GMT Society in May 1974 to reflect the change in operating area of the PTE. It has been at the Manchester Museum of Transport since June 1978.

TNA 520

CHASSIS	LEYLAND TITAN PD2/34	1958
BODY	BURLINGHAM	1958
TYPE	65-SEAT REAR ENTRANCE	

Another Manchester Leyland rear open-platform double-deck bus in preservation is No. 3520, new in September 1958. It was numerically the last of 50 with 65-seat bodywork from Blackpool manufacturer Burlingham, supplier of the Corporation's final trolleybus bodies. The distinctive cantilevered platform design has been abandoned but the body has been modified to meet the then current Manchester specification, which included a more upright front than the normal Burlingham design.

Number 3520 was one of five to be fitted with differing semi- or fully-automatic gearboxes for evaluation when new. It became SELNEC 3520 in November 1969 and passed to the GMPTE in April 1974.

In February 1977 it was purchased for preservation by D. Thrower, then became owned by a preservation group in September 1983. After another change of ownership it was purchased by J. Crankshaw of Meltham, a preservationist with three other PSVs. Mr Crankshaw rotates the garaging of his vehicles between Manchester and Meltham and 3520 went to the Manchester Museum of Transport between May 1979 and March 1987, returning there in September 1993.

The photograph, opposite, shows the vehicle coming down Middleton Road, Manchester, on the Trans-Lancs run which finshes in Manchester's Heaton Park, on the left of this illustration. In days long gone by trams turned into the Park at this point and No. 3520 will run alongside the former tramway sidings where restored Manchester tramcar 765 operates on many Sunday afternoons. A Vintage Bus Service also operates within the Park on special occasions.

ANH 154

CHASSIS	DAIMLER CVG6	1947
BODY	NCB	1947
TYPE	56-SEAT REAR ENTRANCE	

The fluted radiator top of the Daimler still has an imposing air of quality and surviving Daimler buses somehow convey an impression of refinement and quality.

Northampton Corporation Transport introduced electric tramcars on 21st July 1904, replacing the horse trams it had purchased on 21st October 1901.

On 13th September 1923 it introduced motor buses, placing five Thornycroft J type single-deck buses with Brush-built bodies into service.

During 1924 and 1925 further Thornycrofts arrived. Between 1926 and 1930 Guys became the favourite make, these being followed by a variety of AEC, Crossley, Dennis and Vulcan buses, Crossley becoming the favoured make in the early 'thirties.

In 1936 two double-deck buses were bought for evaluation, one each from Leyland and Daimler. The Corporation was looking for the buses which its former tram drivers would find the easiest to handle.

Daimlers were selected and in the next 36 years only eleven out of the 183 buses purchased were not of that make. Equally consistent was the body policy with 120 of the 183 buses having Roe-built conventional rear-entrance bodywork.

Although Northampton was obviously a staunch Roe supporter, by good fortune the surviving example carries an example of a much rarer make of body. Number 154 was one of the Daimler CVG6 models with Gardner 6LW engines and preselective gearboxes purchased in 1947 with a 56-seat body built by Northern Coach Builders of Newcastle when Roe could not deliver without unacceptable delay. NCB was not a large company but after the war was successful in obtaining a number of orders at a time when supplies of material were difficult to obtain.

When Daimler 154 was taken out of service in October 1964 it became a driver training bus until December 1973 when it was placed into store. Between May 1976 and May

1978 it was used as a 'Publicity Bus' after a certain amount of renovation by Northampton Transport. It then returned to store, being taken over by Northampton Transport Ltd in October 1986. In April 1990 it was purchased for preservation by the 154 Preservation Society.

It is seen in April 1995 at the Cobham Bus Museum annual open day organised by the London Bus Preservation Trust. This event includes a free bus service operated by Vintage Buses between Cobham Museum, Brooklands Museum and other sites.

The Nottingham Corporation Act 1899 gave the Corporation powers to construct and operate electric tramways and electric trams replaced horse trams on the Sherwood route on 1st January 1901. The first electric tramway was abandoned on 10th April 1927 when trolleybuses replaced the Nottingham Road trams. After the 1935 conversions to trolleybuses the remaining tram routes were converted to buses. The last tram ran on 5th September 1936.

When the original 1927-8 trolleybuses had been withdrawn in 1936 Nottingham City Transport's trolleybuses were all 60 or 64-seat three-axle models, built by Karrier, Leyland and Ransomes. During the war Nottingham acquired thirteen second-hand vehicles from Cleethorpes, Southend and Hastings as well as a demonstrator which Daimler still had in stock.

The Ministry of War Transport allocated five of the 25 Sunbeam two-axle trolleybuses which could not be shipped to Johannesburg, South Africa, to Nottingham in 1942. Special dispensation was given to operate them since at 8ft wide they were 6in wider than the legal limit.

A further 35 M. o W .T.-allocated Karrier W4 trolleybuses with utility bodies were received from 1943 to 1946. In 1948 a further four Karrier two-axle W4 model trolleybuses arrived, this time with attractive Roe bodies to peacetime standards. To replace all the pre-war trolleybuses and the second-hand acquisitions Nottingham ordered a fleet of thirteen two-axle model 9611T and 102 three-axle model 9641T trolleybuses from British United Traction Ltd.

BUT was formed in late 1946 by Leyland Motors Ltd and Associated Equipment Co Ltd to take over the trolleybus activities of both companies. It was to undertake the design, manufacture and servicing of all types of trolleybuses.

Number 506, KTV 506, is one of the 25 8ft-wide BUT model 9641T trolleybuses supplied with Brush bodies. The other seventy-seven 9641T model trolleybuses had similar Brush bodies but were only 7ft 6in wide. They had been ordered some time before the Ministry of Transport allowed the general use of 8ft vehicles in 1950. Before this, operators could only use the wider examples on authorised routes which the Traffic Commissioners had to approve.

Brush Electrical Engineering Co Ltd owned by the BET group had built thousands of trams and bus bodies for associated companies as well as other customers. It had built trolleybuses for the National Electric Company at Mexborough and Rhondda pre-1914 in addition to three for Stockport.

In the 1930s it again tried to enter the trolleybus market using Thornycroft chassis frames. After the boom years of the late 1940s Brush withdrew from body building activities in 1952 to concentrate production on diesel railway traction equipment and locomotives. Its bodybuilding and order book went to Willowbrook Ltd of Loughborough.

Number 506, first placed in service in January 1950, was chosen to be the official last trolleybus when the Nottingham trolleybus system closed on 1st July 1966, being specially painted and lettered for the occasion. In May 1967 it was purchased by the Huddersfield Trolleybus Preservation Society with help from J. Airey and M. Storry, ownership changing to West Riding Trolleybus Society in November 1968 and in 1970 to West Riding Transport Society which in turn became the West Riding Transport Circle in May 1974. By January 1991 ownership had been transferred to British Trolleybus Society. It is seen at Sandtoft in 1995.

Motor bus number 161, seen on this page, was a post war delivery from AEC. Delivery of this batch was delayed at the request of the operator and regulations concerning permissable length of buses had changed by the time the chassis were delivered. Park Royal built as per the original specification and the chassis were shortened to suit the earlier specification.

The body is as sound today as when it was built, being a particularly good example of a solidly-constructed Park Royal product. This was not the best period for the London bodybuilder and it is good to see such a fine example flying the flag for what was,

generally, one of the industry's leading bodybuilders.

The buses gave good service in Nottingham, many then being sold to other operators for further service, including Cleethorpes, where they continued to perform sterling service.

The well-kept bus is owned by David Allen and Gavin Bairstow and is housed with a selection of other preserved vehicles at the Ruddington Heritage Centre on the Great Central Railway. It was photographed in the picturesque village centre during Spring 1994.

OTV 161		
CHASSIS	AEC REGENT III	1954
BODY	PARK ROYAL	1954
TYPE	56-SEAT REAR ENTRANCE	

Oldham Corporation operated tramcars between 15th December 1900 and 3rd August 1946, its first three motor buses being placed into service in 1913 as feeders to the tramways. These were Tilling-Stevens 40hp petrol electric open-top double-deck buses seating 34 passengers. Withdrawn in May 1917, all were sold to Warrington Corporation for further use.

Services were continued at Oldham using at least one electric single-deck bus seating 21 passengers and built by Electromobile (Leeds) Ltd. This was used until 13th September 1919 when the services were discontinued.

Oldham Corporation resumed the operation of motor omnibuses in December 1924. In 1925 it provided two trolleybuses for the service jointly worked between Ashton and Oldham which commenced on 26th August 1925 but on 5th September 1926 Oldham withdrew its trolleybuses from the Oldham part of the route.

A variety of Leyland, AEC, Guy and Karrier buses was purchased between 1924 and 1930 but the 1925 AEC double-deck buses were fitted with Roe bodies, a builder which Oldham continued to support with orders until the formation of SELNEC in 1969. Leyland chassis were in the majority from c1931.

Number 394, NBU 494, was new in 1957 and was still in service with SELNEC when GMPTE was formed in 1974. Between 1974 and 1978 it was used as a driver trainer, being the last bus to carry the later Oldham livery of Pommard and cream when withdrawn in 1978.

By 1980 it had been restored by craftsmen at the Oldham depot and from April 1979 it has been on display at the Museum of Transport, Manchester.

It was photographed between its duties when working the one-time Vintage Bus Service within Manchester's Heaton Park.

The practice of painting buses in former tramway liveries has provided opportunities to see liveries long-since replaced and this Plymouth bus is just such an example.

Plymouth Corporation operated electric tramcars between 22nd September 1899 and 29th September 1945, the trams being painted in a red and yellow livery until 1922. Between 1922 and 1927 the livery changed to yellow and cream, then until 1930 a teak livery was applied to the trams. In 1930 the familiar maroon and ivory livery was introduced which continued on motor buses after 1945.

In 1915 the Corporation also took over the trams and the lease of the Devonport and District Tramway Company. Motor buses were introduced on 12th July 1920 when 20 Straker Squire 'A' type 34-seat single-deck buses were placed in service on four routes.

When the war started in 1939 the Corporation's preference was obvious – the fleet comprised 206 Leyland Titans, 7 Dennis Lances, and one AEC Regent double-deck bus and two Leyland Cub single-deck buses.

During the Second World War heavy bombing destroyed large parts of the city centre and vehicles necessitating the purchase of a large number of utility buses mostly of Guy manufacture. With the exception of six Crossleys, all post-war buses were purchased from Leyland until the demise of that supplier.

In 1956 a batch of 24 Leyland PD2/12 double-deck buses with Metro-Cammell bodywork was purchased. In 1961 one of these, No 58, was converted to open-top after receiving extensive roof damage. Its seating capacity was returned to 56 from 59 and, named *Sir Francis Drake,* it was used to take visitors to famous spots such as Plymouth Hoe and Mayflower Steps on a sea front circular route.

In 1970 it was renamed *Captain Christopher Jones,* for one season only, before reverting to its former name whilst in April 1974 it was renumbered 358. Between 1979 and 1983 it was used as a temporary trainer with occasional use on PSV duties. In May 1992 it was repainted in a yellow livery and relettered with 'Plymouth Corporation Tramway' legends to commemorate 100 years of transport and placed back into PSV use. It is now in the care of the Plymouth Transport Interest Group who look after it for its current owner Plymouth City Bus Ltd. It is seen in August 1994 at the Bristol Festival of Transport.

This venerable Thornycroft is one of the oldest preserved buses to be an active participant in the rally scene, being a splendid ambassador for its home town. It also represents a type of vehicle few will remember having seen on the road, and a chassis make which has also become something of a rarity.

Portsmouth Corporation introduced electric trams on 24th September 1901 having purchased the Portsmouth Street Tramways Ltd horse tramway system with effect from midnight on 31st December 1899. The last horse tram ran in May 1903, the electric trams being gradually replaced in turn by trolleybuses introduced in October 1934. The last tram ran in November 1936 and eventually the last trolleybus gave way to the motor bus on 27th July 1963.

Motor buses had first been introduced in July 1919 when ten ex-War Department 40hp Thornycroft 'J' type chassis with 34-seat open-top double-deck bodies built by Wadham Brothers from nearby Waterlooville were bought, each costing the Corporation £1,274.

In 1927 second-hand Dodson 'B' type bodies were purchased from the London General Omnibus Co and fitted to the Thornycroft buses remaining in service. Notice how the body follows stage coach practice which was continued with horse buses and trams whereby the body sits within the rear wheels, producing a narrow saloon and an antiquated appearance.

Number 10, BK 2986 was kept as a service vehicle after being withdrawn from service in the late 1920s until the Corporation restored it as fleet No. 1 at some time in the late 1930s. An early electric tram car was also kept and when the trolleybus sysyem closed an example of that mode of transport was also retained for posterity..

Prior to Portsmouth City Transport Ltd being formed on 26th October 1986, the preserved vehicles were placed in the care of Portsmouth City Museum and between 1991 and 1993 No. 1 was restored once again with assistance from Blue Admiral and given its old number 10. It is seen entering the July 1994 rally held at Royal Victoria Country Park, Southampton.

CHASSIS	LEYLAND PDR2/1	1971
BODY	SEDDON PENNINE	1971
TYPE	40-SEAT FRONT ENTRANCE	

In June 1936 Portsmouth Corporation's passenger transport undertaking was renamed City of Portsmouth Passenger Transport Department.

After a variety of Crossley and Leyland buses purchased in the 1930s, when war came Portsmouth was allocated nine utility Daimler double-deck buses and twelve utility Bedford OWB single-deck buses, both types being delivered with wooden-slatted seats.

After the war Leylands again became the main choice until 1969 although 31 Crossley DD42 double-deck buses were purchased in 1948-9, twelve of these having unusual bodies built by Reading Coachbuilders in Hilsea, a Portsmouth suburb.

When the rear-engined era arrived Portsmouth placed Leyland Atlantean double-deckers and Leyland Panther and AEC Swift single deckers in service. Neither of the single deck types was universally popular and so perhaps it was no surprise that being satisfied with the Atlantean double-deck buses the next twelve standee single-deck buses purchased were Leyland Atlantean PDR2/1 chassis with bodies built by Seddon Pennine at Oldham seating 40 plus 19 standees. They were given fleet numbers 188-199.

The last of these to operate in service was No. 196, new in 1971 and was withdrawn in 1986 when it was sold to the Port Harbour Master at Portsmouth and had its seating capacity reduced to fifteen.

In May 1988 it passed with the Port Contract to Provincial, Gosport which almost immediately sold the vehicle for preservation to K. Young and C. Batten of Gosport who have restored it to its original Portsmouth livery and condition. It too is seen at the July 1994 Royal Victoria Country Park rally in Southampton.

Two other similar Portsmouth Seddon Pennine Atlanteans have survived, No. 190 is preserved by the 190 Group and No. 191 is with the Cadet Corps of the training school of *HMS Nelson.*

HTB 656

CHASSIS	LEYLAND PS1	1946
BODY	ROE	1946
TYPE	35-SEAT REAR ENTRANCE	

The smallest municipal fleet in Lancashire was operated by Ramsbottom Urban District Council with a fleet of 17 – one less than neighbouring Haslingden's 18!

Ramsbottom's first service was operated by trolleybuses which started on 14th August 1913, linking Holcombe Brook railway station with Ramsbottom, Stubbins and Edenfield.

Motor buses were introduced in August 1923 and by 1930 four services were operated, linking Bury with Rawtenstall and beyond, and being co-ordinated jointly by Bury and Rawtenstall Corporations and Ramsbottom UDC. Vehicles used included five Thornycroft and seven Leyland single-deckers and the last trolleybus to remain in service, which was used on a few journeys per day until total withdrawal of the trolleybus service on 31st March 1931.

One of the features of the Ramsbottom fleet for many years was the Council's loyalty to C. H. Roe, the Chief Draughtsman of RET Construction Co Ltd which supplied the first six trolleybuses in 1913-1915. He steered the vehicles as they were towed over the Pennines by traction engine.

Charles Roe went into business for himself after the First World War and the majority of orders for bodywork were placed with him until 1952.

It is therefore appropriate that No. 17, a 1946 Leyland PS1 with Roe 35-seat rear-entrance body survives. After withdrawal in 1968 it was purchased for preservation.

Various changes of ownership followed, culminating in it being restored between May 1978 and June 1983 by GMT at Bury workshops and repainted in Ramsbottom maroon livery. It was then loaned to the British Commercial Vehicle Museum at Leyland, returning to the Manchester Museum of Transport in September 1988. In September 1993 it went on loan to the Bury Transport Museum, returning in 1995 to the Boyle Street museum, in an arrangement designed to promote increased interest in both organisations.

TTD 386H

CHASSIS	LEYLAND PD3/14	1969
BODY	EAST LANCS	1969
TYPE	73-SEAT FORWARD ENTRANCE	

When SELNEC was formed in October 1969, taking over in November 1969 eleven municipalities in Greater Manchester, the Ramsbottom Council's fleet was included. The fleet, by then only twelve strong and numbered 1-12 became in due course SELNEC 6401 to 6411 and 6082 respectively.

The most unusual vehicle was No. 12 which was purchased third-hand from Warrington Corporation in December 1967 which had used it from December 1965, initially on hire, until January 1966 when it was purchased from Halifax Joint Omnibus Committee. This became SELNEC No. 6082 and was the only Albion Nimbus model NS3AN to be used by SELNEC. It carried a 31-seat Weymann body and had been purchased to replace the Leyland Tiger No. 17 shown on page 56 (opposite) when that vehicle was sold into preservation.

The most noteworthy, however, was Ramsbottom No. 11, the last traditional half-cab bus built for use in Britain and the last exposed radiator bus to be built in the UK. This was also the last Leyland Titan PD3 chassis to leave the Leyland works in early 1969, having been built in late 1968. It had been delivered to Ramsbottom as fleet No. 11 but had not entered service when SELNEC took charge in November 1969.

After a successful and relatively untroubled existence Greater Manchester PTE withdrew it from service in April 1981 and placed it on loan to the Museum of Transport in Manchester.

It has been restored back into the Ramsbottom UDC colours of maroon and white and with its attractive East Lancs 73-seat body is a reminder of the smallest Lancashire municipality.

It is seen in GMT livery shortly after a normal repaint whilst still in service.

EMMER GREEN

47

RD 7127

RD 7127

CHASSIS	AEC REGENT	1935
BODY	PARK ROYAL	1935
TYPE	52-SEAT REAR ENTRANCE	

Pre-war double-deckers always catch the eye and this Reading AEC Regent is no exception.

Reading Corporation acquired the horse tramway undertaking of the Reading Tramway Company at the end of October 1901, operating horse cars until electric trams were introduced on 22nd July 1903.

The first motor bus service was introduced on 6th December 1919 when two AEC 'YC' type motor buses with open-top double-deck bus bodies entered service on a route between Tilehurst and Caversham Heights.

Trolleybuses introduced on 18th July 1936 replaced trams on a trial route between Caversham and Whitley. The success of this trial led to the replacement of the main line route from Earley to Tilehurst and London Road to Norcot Road Junction with trolleybuses on 21st May 1939. Trolleybus routes were in turn replaced by motor buses between 10th July 1965 and 3rd November 1968, when the last one was withdrawn.

It is appropriate that one of the 1935 AEC Regents, No. 47, with an early example of a metal-framed Park Royal body, has survived long enough for it to be secured for preservation. It was withdrawn from service on 29th February 1956 and was sold to Lancashire Motor Traders in January 1957. In October 1957 it was sold to A. G. Linfield Ltd, of Thakeham for use as staff transport.

In October 1963 it was purchased by Reading Transport Society for preservation, ownership being transferred to the British Trolleybus Society in April 1971.

It is seen operating on the vintage bus service at the April 1995 Cobham Bus Museum Open Day, organised by the London Bus Preservation Trust. In keeping with many events held in 1995 to commemorate the 50th anniversary of VE and VJ day, it had been suitably modified with white-tipped mudguards and guard rails which were necessary additions during the war when vehicles had to be driven with hardly any illumination. The white markings helped to give warning of the vehicle's prescence.

HDK 835

CHASSIS	AEC REGENT III	1951
BODY	EAST LANCS	1951
TYPE	59-SEAT REAR ENTRANCE	

Restoring and repainting a preserved bus is a long job and much preparation is necessary to obtain the excellent finish which typifies old vehicles. Rubbing down such large areas of paint is not for the faint-hearted as can be imagined from this picture.

An interesting aspect of municipal liveries was the way in which a manager sometimes took 'his' livery with him when he moved to another undertaking. Rochdale appointed G. A. Cherry as its manager in 1935, and he changed the former light brown and orange livery to a blue and cream scheme similar to that at Rotherham – his previous undertaking.

Mr Cherry moved to become manager of Birkenhead's transport department during the war and in 1946 four vehicles arrived there in Rochdale livery, but they were quickly repainted in Birkenhead's standard colour scheme.

Rochdale Corporation operated electric trams between 22nd May 1902 and 12th November 1932, whilst motorbuses were first introduced on 17th March 1926 on the Castleton route.

The Corporation participated in the express service linking Manchester with Rochdale which started on 24th October 1927. This service was extended at both ends, in 1927 and 1928, to provide express services linking Bacup to Flixton, and Littleborough with Altrincham. The Bacup route, at 26.7 miles long, was the longest of the Manchester area express services which were an important feature of the transport network in the 'twenties.

After the implementation of the 1930 Road Traffic Act in January 1931 the long express bus services crossing Manchester were curtailed after pressure from the Railway companies.

During the 1930s AEC, Crossley, Daimler, Dennis and Leyland vehicles were purchased. A number of these carried Craven-built bodies which had become popular in operations where the LMS Railway had an interest.

The post-war fleet consisted of AEC Regent III double-

deck buses with Weymann or East Lancs bodies as well as fifteen AEC Regent IV single-deck buses with East Lancs and Burlingham bodies. Four of these were sold in 1957 to Lancaster Corporation. There had also been some second-hand AEC buses from Halifax and Sheffield.

In 1953 30 Daimler CVG6 double-deck buses were purchased. Clearly impressed with their Gardner 6LW engines, Rochdale was one of the few municipalities to purchase AEC Regent Vs with Gardner 6LW units, 40 arriving in 1956.

One of the 1951 AEC Regents has survived into preservation. Fleet No. 235, new in September 1951, carries a 59-seat East Lancs body. It was withdrawn in March 1969 and was bought for preservation by G. Bottomley, one of the founder members of Transiclub which organised vintage vehicle rallies in Rochdale from 1967 until the late 'seventies.

In December 1989 it was sold to Steve Lord of Manchester and was at Manchester's Museum of Transport, Boyle Street in 1993 before being moved to one of the store locations used by the museum for restoration to continue.

BBA 560

CHASSIS	AEC REGENT	1939
BODY	PARK ROYAL	1939
TYPE	48-SEAT REAR ENTRANCE	

Salford Corporation purchased a portion of the horse tramway and rolling stock of the Manchester Carriage and Tramway Co on 27th April 1901 when the Compaany's lease expired in Salford, and started to convert the lines to be suitable for electric traction. The first electric trams were introduced on 4th October 1901, between Blackfriars Bridge and Kersal via Bury New Road. Initially Salford's cars were excluded from Manchester and it was not until 31st May 1903 that Salford cars could travel along Deansgate in Manchester, subject to a rental payment to compensate Manchester for loss of revenue on their trams.

Salford introduced motor buses on 5th July 1920 on a tramway feeder service linking Pendleton with Great Cheetham Street. Leyland chassis remained the favourite purchase until late 1923 after which in 1927 Salford was one of the first municipalities to introduce three-axle buses built by Karrier Motors Ltd of Huddersfield. By 1928 the fleet had grown to 36 buses.

During the 1930s Salford applied a multi-sourcing policy for new vehicles, Dennis vehicles being popular at one stage. The 1939 purchases included both AEC and Leyland chassis with a mixture of bodies from four suppliers.

Salford's electric trams were replaced with motor buses progressively from the early 1930s until 31st March 1947.

Two of the ten AEC Regent buses with 8.8-litre A180 engines, crash gearboxes and 48-seat Park Royal bodies from 1939 were converted into dual-control instruction vehicles when post-war replacements arrived in 1948. One of the these, No 98, former bus No. 235, was still in use in November 1969 when SELNEC took over the Salford fleet.

After withdrawal in 1970 it was purchased for preservation in 1971 by R. Marshall and P. Edginton. Since then the dual-control equipment has been removed and the bus has been restored externally to its original pre-war red and white livery by craftsmen at the former Frederick Road works of Salford Corporation.

Since its restoration in the mid-1970s, No. 235 has been on display at the Museum of Transport in Manchester, its present owners. Some renovation of the platform area has taken place and the vehicle awaits a full set of seats since the originals were rermoved when the conversion to dual-control took place.

The photograph was taken outside the former offices at Frederick Road depot, the vehicle's original home. This famous building, like so many former transport complexes, became redundant and has been demolished. Happily the ornamental arch has been left standing as a reminder of the site's importance in days gone by.

TRJ 112

CHASSIS	DAIMLER CVG6	1962
BODY	MCW	1962
TYPE	65-SEAT REAR ENTRANCE	

Many of the services had continued to run through the war years with consequential problems for both the tram and bus fleets. Salford had many more buses than it actually needed but due to lack of spares and staff during the bleak war years it had difficulty in maintaining services and was in constant difficulties with the Ministry of Transport from 1941 who could not understand why in a fleet of 225 vehicles, 70 could be defective and since some 160 buses were needed to maintain services the manager, Mr J. W. Blakemore, was subjected to severe criticism. After he retired in mid-1946 Salford had difficulty in appointing a replacement manager to take over a fleet of trams and buses which in many cases were incapable of being in service all day.

Eventually the new manager, Mr C. W. Baroth, appointed in August 1946, introduced a number of hired and second-hand vehicles in 1946-7 and was able to replace the last trams. With the arrival of some 343 Crossley, AEC, Leyland and Daimler buses between 1947 and 1953 he eliminated the pre-war bus fleet. This in turn started to be replaced in 1962 when the next 50 vehicles arrived, comprising ten AEC Reliances (one with a coach body), and 30 Daimler CVG6 double-deck buses with 65-seat Metropolitan-Cammell Orion style bodies with conventional open rear platforms. The other ten buses were six front-entrance 64-seat Daimler CVG6 and for evaluation two Daimler Fleetlines and two Leyland Atlanteans. The latter four allowed the Salford City Transport Department to compare rear-engined double-deck buses from the two manufacturers. Interestingly only five more Daimlers were purchased by Salford, the other 168 being Leylands!

It was appropriate that the last survivor of the 30 1962 Daimlers, Salford No. 112, SELNEC and GMPTE 4001 was purchased in May 1977 by E. Gray for preservation after withdrawal, ownership passing to D. Harris and others in August 1986. By June 1995 it was in the care of D. Cooper and K. Platt.

Since June 1978 it has been displayed at the Museum of Transport, Manchester and is a splendid reminder of the 'Baroth' period when the excellent standard of turn-out of Salford's hand-painted buses in 'Salford Green' and cream became the norm for all vehicles unlike neighbouring fleets.

Number 112 is seen at the September 1994 rally organised by the Greater Manchester Transport Society in Heaton Park.

657 BWB

CHASSIS	LEYLAND ATLANTEAN	1962
BODY	PARK ROYAL	1967
TYPE	77-SEAT FRONT ENTRANCE	

Sheffield's horse tramway, introduced in 1873, was acquired by Sheffield Corporation in 1896 and electrified between 1899 and 1902. Motor bus services commenced in February 1913 and continued to expand in and around Sheffield until December 1928 when, under the powers granted to them, the LMS and LNE railways acquired the long-distance services operated by the Corporation and entered into an agreement with the Corporation to coordinate services in the area. Starting in 1929, therefore, Sheffield Corporation operated three fleets of buses all painted in its livery. The 'A' fleet operated Corporation-only routes within the city boundary. The 'B' fleet was operated by the Corporation on behalf of the Joint Omnibus Committee in which the Corporation had a half share, with both the LMSR and the LNER having a quarter share each. The 'C' fleet was operated by the Corporation on behalf of the two railway companies.

When the railways were nationalised in January 1948 the British Transport Commission became the Corporation's partner.

When the 1968 Transport Act became law Sheffield tried to acquire the interests then held by the British Railways Board. The 'B' fleet was acquired one hundred per cent by the Corporation but it took only a few of the 'C' fleet services, the rest passing to National Bus Company subsidiaries.

The South Yorkshire municipalities of Sheffield, Rotherham and Doncaster were acquired on 1st April 1974 by the South Yorkshire Passenger Transport Executive. The liveries of many of these municipalities can be seen at the Sheffield Bus Museum at Tinsley depot.

Others can be found elsewhere and one of these is 657 BWB which was new in April 1962 as fleet No. 1357, a 'B' fleet vehicle which when new carried a Weymann 77-seat body on its Leyland Atlantean PDR1/1 rear-engined chassis. In July 1967 that body was destroyed by fire and the chassis was reconditioned before it was rebodied with a new Park Royal body, seen here, with the same seating arrangement.

When Sheffield Corporation gained control of the 'B' fleet, No 1357 was renumbered in June 1970 becoming No. 227. In April 1974 it passed to SYPTE and then between July 1978 and December 1985 was used as a driver trainer.

In January 1986 it was purchased by the Sheffield Transport Group from Doncaster for preservation. It is normally kept at the Sandoft Trolleybus Museum where it was seen in July 1995 at the annual Sandoft gathering resplendently restored into the Sheffield livery carrying fleet number 1357.

UMA 370

CHASSIS	ATKINSON PD 746	1955
BODY	NORTHERN COUNTIES	1955
TYPE	60-SEAT CENTRE ENTRANCE	

This vehicle can rightly claim to be unique. It is the only double-decker bus produced by Atkinson, and was built at a time when the company was making inroads into the underfloor-engined single-decker market.

SHMD began operating Gardner-engined Atkinson single-deckers in 1954 and the transport department manager, Mr Stockton, had persuaded the manufacturer to produce a double-decker. The chassis was displayed in the demonstration area at the 1954 Commercial Motor Show and was then sent to Northern Counties, SHMD's exclusive bodybuilder, for completion. It was fitted with the centre-entrance body shown, that being the SHMD standard of the time and arrived in newly adopted lighter green livery.

SHMD– the famous Stalybridge, Hyde, Mossley and Dukinfield Transport and Electricity Board, usually known as SHMD Joint Board – operated electric tramways between 21st May 1904 and 19th May 1945. Motor bus services began on 29th May 1925 using eight Vickers-bodied Thornycroft single-deckers. The Thornycroft association continued until 1937 when the manufacturer ceased building buses. Daimler then became the exclusive make for several years.

The Atkinson double-decker was destined to be a one-off. Its central staircase location, matching the centre-entrance, can be seen by the window configuration in this illustration. The vehicle was modified by the removal of one seat in 1966 but otherwise remained as built, giving good service until it was withdrawn by GMT in 1970. Its importance was recognised and it immediately passed into the care of the Manchester Museum of Transport where it can still be found.

It was photographed on an enthusiasts' day in 1995, working a vintage bus service from Manchester to Droylsden in connection with the 75th Anniversary of Maynes, the Manchester independent.

One of the similarly-bodied SHMD Daimlers also survives in preservation. It displays the earlier dark green livery.

construction on 19th September 1921. New and regular services were commenced on 17th August 1923.

Trolleybuses were introduced on a route which commenced at Rainhill, two miles out of town, and ran to Prescot, starting on 11th July 1927. The last trolleybus ran on 1st July 1958 when No. 374 ceremoniously closed the system which had contracted to just one route – St. Helens, Prescot and Rainhill loop – normal services having ceased to operate on 30th June. The last sixteen trolleybuses were sold for further service with the eight Sunbeams going to South Shields and the eight BUTs to Bradford.

The St. Helens bus fleet had expanded in June 1922 when the services and vehicles of the St. Helens and District Motor Service were acquired. By 1929 the motor bus fleet comprised 29 single-deck buses of Guy, Leyland, Bristol and Daimler manufacture.

St Helens was one of many operators constrained by the location of low railway bridges which affected its services. The Corporation's first double-deck motor buses, four Leyland-bodied Leyland TD1 lowbridge, were placed in service in 1931, followed by similar vehicles in 1932 and 1933 from Crossley and Leyland. A selection of vehicle makes and types followed, including second hand examples from Wigan.

In 1949 a new general manager, R. Edgeley Cox, was appointed and recognising the problems caused by many of the low bridges in St. Helens, he was able to persuade the Corporation to purchase the more expensive AEC Regent RT double-deck bus which London Transport used. This type of bus was 2½ins lower in height than the traditional highbridge double-deck buses then being built for provincial use. He ordered 40 of this type which enabled many more passengers to travel in comfort in buses with conventional double seats on either side of a central gangway upstairs, which was not possible on lowbridge double-deck buses with bench seats for four passengers only accessible from the offside sunken gangway.

When these 40 buses were withdrawn from service in St. Helens, nineteen of them were purchased by Kingston-

BDJ 67

CHASSIS	AEC REGENT III RT	1950
BODY	PARK ROYAL	1950
TYPE	56-SEAT REAR ENTRANCE	

St Helens was a small but interesting operator but one of its greatest claims to fame was its purchase of new AEC RT vehicles to full London specification. The choice was largely made because, despite being of normal seating configuration, as opposed to side-gangway layout, the vehicles were low enough to pass below St Helens' infamous railway bridges.

St. Helens Corporation had taken over the operation of the local company's tramway system on 1st October 1919 and then in 1921 obtained powers to operate motor buses which were introduced on certain tramway routes under

-upon-Hull Corporation for further use. One of the first batch of fifteen– BDJ 59-73, No 67 new in June 1950, has been preserved. It is a fitting memorial to Edgeley Cox's acumen, and his Transport Committee's support, for although many operators purchased second-hand RTs and obtained good service from them, only St. Helens purchased new examples.

In 1952 R. Edgeley Cox moved to Walsall and was succeeded by Mr J. C. Wake who introduced prefix letters to the fleet numbers to identify groups of vehicles; thus plain number 67 became D67. In October 1962 it was one of the vehicles sold to Kingston-upon-Hull Corporation where it was used it until December 1970.

After withdrawal from service in Hull the vehicle was purchased for preservation and after passing through several hands is now owned by G. Sandford. It was placed in the care of the St. Helens Trolleybus Transport Society and is now one of the exhibits at the St. Helens Transport Museum.

EDJ 244J

CHASSIS	AEC SWIFT	1971
BODY	MARSHALL	1971
TYPE	44-SEAT DUAL DOOR	

Our second St Helens vehicle comes from a much later period. AEC Swift number 244 was delivered to the Corporation in 1971, after the formation of Merseyside PTE into which the undertaking was to pass, but before the boundary changes of the Local Government Reorganisation became effective in 1974.

The Swift, like the Lowestoft vehicle shown on page 44, is a rear engined model and St Helens had 66 of these in stock, with a further nine on order, out of the fleet of 127 buses which passed to the PTE in 1974.

The single-deckers were fitted with standee bodies by Marshall of Cambridge, except for three which had been acquired second-hand from Lancashire United and carried Northern Counties bodies.

Clearly the Swift found favour with St Helens but this was not always the case. Number 224 has been restored to a high standard by its owner, a former MTL Manchester engineer, and provides a reminder of one of AEC's more controversial models.

Whilst the chassis was not universally respected there was no doubt that the Marshall body was very popular, particularly in BET company fleets, and could be seen widely throughout the country. The bright St Helens livery shows it at its best at an AEC Society rally.

LOW 217

CHASSIS	GUY ARAB III	1954
BODY	PARK ROYAL	1954
TYPE	56-SEAT REAR ENTRANCE	

Southampton Corporation started operating motor buses in 1900 but, unlike Eastbourne which started in 1903 and continued without a break, Southampton's operation was not continuous.

In 1900 Southampton hired a Granville 11-seat motor wagonette and used it on a trial service between 1st and 8th August 1900. Encouraged by the trials Southampton then placed orders for three Daimler 12-seat vehicles, the first entering service on 5th August 1901. The erratic performance of this vehicle caused the service to be withdrawn on 20th December 1901 and as only one Daimler had been delivered it was returned to the manufacturer and the order for the other two was cancelled.

Attempts were made to try again with motor buses in 1914, but the war prevented this. Eventually, on 31st July 1919, motor bus services were reintroduced using a fleet of Thornycroft buses. In 1926 the Corporation purchased its first Guy-built vehicles; by 1939 the fleet was predominantly Leyland and then after the loss of vehicles during the wartime air raids eight Ministry of War Transport-allocated Guy Arabs entered the fleet in 1944.

The wartime Arab was an extremely reliable chassis, if somewhat basic. It made a favourable impression in many fleets where Guys would have been unheard of before the war, or others like Southampton where the make had made only a small impact. In the next twelve years all buses purchased by the Corporation were Gardner-engined Guys, all with bodies built by Park Royal.

Many of these were used to replace the remaining electric tramcars which had been introduced in Southampton on 22nd January 1900 and operated until 31st December 1949.

The last of the 175 Guy Arab III double-deck buses arrived in 1954 and the last one to operate in service, No. 71, LOW 217 was withdrawn in June 1975 after being in service since September 1954. It was retained by the Transport Department for preservation and the 7164 group from Eastleigh,

Eastleigh, Hampshire, was allowed to take it to rallies and other special events.

In October 1986 ownership of this historic vehicle was transferred to Southampton City Council when the Transport Department became 'City Bus'. In March 1995, after being fully restored to PCV standards, it was placed on loan to City Bus who placed it back into service on special duties.

Some post-war Arabs carried the Indian's head on the radiator filler cap but the Southampton vehicles had the plain, though distinctive, type fitted here. The front mudguards on Guy vehicles were also a very distinctive feature, lacking the subtlety of Leyland and AEC models.

It is seen at the April 1995 Cobham Bus Museum Open Day organised by the London Bus Preservation Trust. In keeping with many events held in 1995 to commemorate the 50th anniversary of VE and VJ day, No. 71's livery of red and cream with the roof being painted silver, which had been introduced in October 1945 and based on pre-war London Transport practice, was suitably modified by the addition of white-edged mudguards and guard rails as had been the pratice in wartime. The pre-war Southampton livery had been an impressive dark blue and cream, lined in gold.

BOW 507C

CHASSIS	AEC REGENT V	1965
BODY	EAST LANCS	1965
TYPE	66-SEAT REAR ENTRANCE	

When Southampton Corporation started to replace its early post-war bus fleet it purchased both Leyland PD2 and AEC Regent V buses, all with rear open platforms. Fleet No. 371 seen on this page (also at Cobham) entered service in March 1965. Southampton had been elevated to city status in 1964 and, accordingly, its buses thereafter carried City of Southampton markings.

Number 371 is an AEC Regent V type 2D3RA with body built by East Lancashire Coachbuilders' Sheffield subsidiary company – Neepsend Coachworks – with seating for 66 passengers. This high figure was achieved by fitting a rear-facing bench seat behind the lower saloon front bulkhead.

The bus entered service in March 1965 and in February 1979 was renumbered 100 after being painted in a blue centenary livery. In December 1979 it was withdrawn from service and retained for preservation by the Transport Department. In March 1985 the bus was renumbered 371 after refurbishment and having been returned into the livery introduced in 1963 where the upper-deck window pillars and the whole of the roof were painted cream.

In October 1986 it passed back into Southampton City Council ownership when, as recorded on the previous pages, the Transport Department became City Bus. In March 1995 it was loaned to City Bus who placed it back into service on special duties.

As the morning sun catches it in service at Cobham it conveys an impression of a vehicle that is being well looked after and will give much pleasure during the day to passengers visiting the different sites.

LCU 112

CHASSIS	DAIMLER CCG6	1964
BODY	ROE	1964
TYPE	63-SEAT REAR ENTRANCE	

South Shields Corporation obtained powers in 1905 to work the former horse tramways in the town, which ceased to run on 1st February 1906. The gauge of the tramways was changed to 4ft 8½in from 3ft 6in, the first electric car running on 30th March 1906. By 1907 there were 35 trams in operation.

Motor buses were introduced on 30th July 1914 between the Stanhope Road tram terminus and Simonside, the two vehicles used being Edison Accumulator buses. In 1919 these were replaced with petrol-engined motor buses, further tramway extensions being constructed during the 1920s. In 1928-9 the Corporation named a number of tramcars, No. 49 becoming *Caer Urfa*, the town's Roman name, and No. 50 being named *Nelson* after the then new battleship.

By 1934 the bus fleet had expanded to ten vehicles. The first of the trams were replaced by trolleybuses on 12th October 1936 with the last trams being replaced on 1st April 1946.

The trolleybus system was replaced with motor buses between 1958 and 29th April 1964. After the five Guy Arab IV buses purchased in 1958, ten Daimler CSG6 models followed, and then the last three batches totalling 39 buses, were Daimler CCG6 with Guy four-speed constant mesh gearboxes and Manchester style new look fronts. All carried 63-seat Roe bodies.

One of the last batch of eighteen, No. 140, LCU 112, new in April 1964, has been restored as a South Shields vehicle. In January 1970 it had passed to Tyneside PTE when Newcastle and South Shields lost their municipal bus fleets. It was then renumbered in the PTE fleet, becoming No. 340. In April 1974 Tyneside PTE was merged with Sunderland's fleet to become Tyne and Wear PTE. In July 1974 the bus was renumbered to 572. In late 1976 it was withdrawn from service and in April 1977 it was loaned to the South Shields

Preservation Group who rallied it. In April 1983 it was placed back in service after restoration to full PSV standard.

In October 1986 it became the property of Busways Travel Services Ltd when the bus operations of the PTE were bought by the management. Number 140 continues to

be used for special duties and also to be rallied by the South Shields group – employees of Busways as the company was before the Stagecoach takeover – and it is seen here at the Gateshead Metro Centre in what must be its nearest rally to home territory.

Atkinson was a builder of underfloor-engined single-decker bus chassis between the early 'fifties and 1964, also building the unique double-decker supplied to SHMD and illustrated on page 63. Few Atkinson examples survive but the chromed emblem on the front of the vehicles is an instant source of identification.

Sunderland municipalised the town's horse tramways in 1900 and electrified them, the first electric Corporation tram running on 15th August 1900.

On 6th February 1928 the tramway service to the docks was replaced with motorbuses which were provided and worked by the Northern General Transport Co Ltd under a working arrangement with the Corporation which continued until May 1930 when the Corporation's first motor buses arrived, these being Leyland Lion model LT1 single-deck buses with Leyland 32-seat bodies. One of these, No. 2 (not shown), is now preserved in its original chocolate and cream livery by Mr M. Plunkett, who keeps it in the South of England. In late 1937 the bus livery was changed to red and cream.

The town's tramway system continued to expand until 1949 but then in 1950 a progressive programme of tramway abandonment was started which was completed on 1st October 1954 when the last tram made its final journey.

The replacing buses were painted in a new green and cream livery to distinguish them from other operators in the area.

During the 1960s the Corporation's Manager, Mr Norman Morton, introduced pay-as-you-enter operation on routes using single-deck buses. In late 1963 and early 1964 three Atkinson Alpha model PM 746HL single-deck buses with dual-door Marshall bodies seating 45 passengers were purchased.

These were the last Atkinson passenger vehicles to be built for use in Britain and carried fleet numbers 46 to 48. All three were still in service when the Sunderland Corporation bus fleet became part of Tyne and Wear PTE in April 1974. Two have since been preserved, the last one, No. 48, being renumbered 848 in July 1974 and then 1848 in 1977.

In August 1977 it was withdrawn from service and placed on loan, as Sunderland No. 48, to Tyne and Wear County Council Museums for display at the Monkwearmouth Station Museum. In 1980 it returned to the Tyne and Wear PTE and was cared for by Sunderland Bus Preservation Group which was composed mainly of PTE employees.

In October 1986 it became the property of Busways Travel Services Ltd, when the bus operations of the PTE were bought by the management, and continues to be in the care of the Busways Bus Preservation Group.

In September 1966 General Manager Norman Morton introduced a token/flat fare system to Sunderland's network of bus services, with many more services being operated by a driver only. Mr Morton had placed a large fleet of rear-engined dual-door single-deck buses into service, built to his specification which included sloping window pillars to make them distinctive. This new fleet included 33 Leyland Panther model PSUR1/1 and three Daimler Roadliners, all 36 being fitted with Strachan 47-seat dual-door bodies.

Panthers and Roadliners were far from popular, engine failures and, more seriously, body fractures due to the weight of the rear mounted engines being not uncommon. By contrast the Bristol RE, against which they were designed to compete, was relatively trouble free and became a very popular chassis indeed.

One of these distinctive Sunderland vehicles, No. 53, new in July 1966, has been preserved. It is one of the Leyland Panthers and after take-over by Tyne and Wear PTE in April 1974 it was twice renumbered – first to 853 in July 1974 and then to 1853 in 1977.

It was withdrawn from service in August 1977 and stored until August 1978 when it was placed into the care of the local Sunderland Bus Preservation Group. In March 1978 it was reinstated as a PSV, becoming Sunderland number 53 once again. In July 1980 it was again withdrawn from service and was still in the care of the group when the Tyne and Wear PTE bus company was bought by the management.

The new company duly became Busways Travel Services Limited, and, accordingly, the preservation group was then renamed the Busways Bus Preservation Group.

The Panther is seen some way from home, at the Bristol rally on a rather dull day in 1994.

CHASSIS	DAIMLER CVG6/30	1967
BODY	NORTHERN COUNTIES	1967
TYPE	70-SEAT FORWARD ENTRANCE	

Swindon was a town which expanded rapidly after the Great Western Railway built its large engineering and railway workshops there in 1841.

By 1904 three short electric tramway routes radiating from the railway station had been built by Swindon Corporation, the total mileage of the three routes being only 3.7 miles, and services commenced on 22nd September 1904 using seven trams which were painted in a maroon and cream livery. By 1921 the fleet had expanded to thirteen cars.

Motor bus services started on 15th April 1927 and the last tram ran on 11th July 1929. By the end of 1929 the Corporation was operating 38 buses on nine routes, the fleet comprising three 30-seat Guy saloons, sixteen Leyland Lion PLSC1 and PLSC3 single-deck buses and nineteen Leyland Titan 48-seat double-deck buses.

Swindon Corporation was the first operator to be allocated one of the Guy Arab utility double-deck buses, in 1942, by the Ministry of War Transport. This vehicle (not illustrated) is now preserved by Thamesdown Borough. Between 1947 and 1961 the Corporation standardised on Daimler buses. After trying small batches of Leyland Titans, Leopards and AEC Reliances, between 1962 and 1964, Daimlers returned in 1967 when four CVG6-30 70-seat double-deck buses were bought with Northern Counties-built bodies.

In April 1974 Thamesdown Transport became responsible for a larger area which absorbed the Swindon Corporation fleet. Number 145, JAM 145E, is still owned as a PCV and is used for special duties by Thamesdown, being restored in the Swindon Corporation livery of blue and cream which was originally introduced in the late 1930s.

It was photographed whilst being displayed at the Bristol Festival of Transport event held in August 1994.

GWU 12

CHASSIS	LEYLAND TITAN PD2/1	1948
BODY	LEYLAND LOWBRIDGE	1948
TYPE	53-SEAT REAR ENTRANCE	

This Leyland body outline for both highbridge, and, as seen here, lowbridge, buses was amongst the neatest of all British designs. The side gangway layout, designed to reduce the overall height of the vehicle, had been patented by the company when the original Titan was introduced in 1927.

Todmorden, a small town in the upper Calder Valley of the West Riding of Yorkshire, introduced motor buses on 1st January 1907, the early vehicles, all open-top double-deckers, including two Critchley-Norris, two Leyland, and a Ryknield built in Burton-on-Trent.

By 1919 the Corporation had standardised on Leyland chassis, a make which it was still buying in 1969 when the last new bus was purchased.

In January 1931 Todmorden entered into an agreement with the LMS Railway to operate the fleet on behalf of the Todmorden Joint Omnibus Committee, with each partner owning half the vehicles.

After the war, a large fleet of Leyland Titan PD2 double-deck buses with Leyland lowbridge bodies was purchased, thirty 7ft 6in-wide examples in 1947-50 and then in 1951 a further eight 8ft-wide vehicles which were painted with a cream roof. Between 1951 and 1960 the fleet still included Todmorden's last two pre-war Leyland Titan double-deck buses, so the fleet was very standardised.

The reason for the lowbridge type of bus was the depot which had been built before full-height buses appeared. Leigh Corporation had the same depot problem!

Several interesting Todmorden vehicles have survived into preservation, the oldest being a 1921 Leyland open-top double-deck bus owned by Mike Sutcliffe. The photograph shows Leyland Titan PD2/1 number 2, fitted with Leyland lowbridge bodywork seating 53.

New in February 1948 it was withdrawn from service in July 1970 and was transferred out of the JOC fleet to the Corporation, which then placed it on loan to the Todmorden Antiquarian Society. Its custodian, B. Newsome of Halifax, kept it at the West Yorkshire Transport Museum, Ludlam Street depot in Bradford between October 1984 and July 1995 when it was moved to a farm in Todmorden in which the Antiquarian Society has an interest.

OED 217

CHASSIS	FODEN PVD6	1956
BODY	EAST LANCS	1956
TYPE	58-SEAT REAR ENTRANCE	

Preserved Foden buses are very few and far between and accordingly this smart Warrington example always arouses interest at rallies. A distinctive feature of the Foden is its speedometer, mounted in the centre of the steering column.

The Lancashire town of Warrington obtained powers to construct a tramway system in 1900, the first service commencing on 21st April 1902.

In 1913 the Corporation introduced three Tilling-Stevens petrol-electric open-top double-deck buses on two services which commenced on 3rd July 1913. Two similar second-hand buses were purchased from Oldham Corporation in 1917.

The next bus route did not start until 1928 and by 1930 only eleven buses were in the fleet, including seven Leyland Leviathan 52-seat top-covered double-deck buses and two low-height AEC type 422 buses with Hall Lewis bodies on solid tyred chassis, an unusual combination. The tram routes were abandoned between 17th September 1931 and 28th August 1935.

Other vehicles bought before the Second World War included AEC Renown three-axle models and various Leyland and Crossley double-deckers. The livery was changed from maroon to red and ivory in 1947.

After the war various Leyland, Guy Arab II and Bristol buses arrived up to November 1948 when the former demonstrator Foden model PVD6 chassis was purchased. Warrington fitted a second-hand body to it from a 1935 Crossley and, satisfied with this, purchased a further fourteen Fodens between 1949 and 1956. The last one to be supplied, fleet No. 112, OED 217 was new in March 1956 and was one of five which had East Lancs 58-seat double-deck bus bodies.

Number 112 was withdrawn in 1972 and in December of that year it was purchased by the Steamport Foden Preservation Group and kept at the Steamport Museum in Southport. In 1984 Alan Pritchard from St. Helens joined the group and since then he has become the owner of No. 112, which is now kept at the St. Helens Bus Museum. Some time after leaving Southport it was stored at Burtonwood with many other preserved vehicles.

In the 1974 Local Government Reorganisation Warrington was moved into Cheshire; was this a thank you to the Corporation for buying fifteen Fodens built at Sandbach in Cheshire? Well it's a pleasant thought!

Centre-entrance double-deckers were far less common than their rear entrance brethren and, accordingly, fewer of them found their way into preservation. This example incorporates the design jointly-patented by Charles H. Roe and the Grimsby Corporation manager and engineer, J. C. Whiteley, and first built for Grimsby in mid-1930. The design incorporated a double staircase.

In 1912 West Hartlepool purchased the tramway system within the borough from the Hartlepool Electric Tramway Co Ltd and also leased the tramway route in Hartlepool, the system being closed by 25th March 1927. Trolleybuses replaced the trams between 28th February 1924 and 25th March 1927, these in turn being withdrawn by 2nd April 1953.

Motor buses were first introduced on 17th July 1920 linking the town with the Tees Transporter Bridge at Port Clarence, across the River Tees from Middlesbrough. By 1929 the Corporation was operating sixteen buses, all being Bristols, many having Roe bodies.

During the 1930s Daimler became the favoured make with the 1937 and 1938 examples having full fronted bodywork and Roe centre-entrance bodies seating 48 passengers.

In 1942 West Hartlepool was fortunate in obtaining an unfrozen Leyland TD7, again with a conventional half-cab design Roe body but still having a centre staircase double-deck body.

Number 36, the preserved example seen here, was new in July 1942. It was withdrawn from service in July 1958 and was used as a driver trainer until purchased for preservation in December 1962 by R. L. Kell of Durham.

It was then stored on a farm at Stokesley in North Yorkshire, subsequently at Burtonwood from 1978 to 1981, and since then at the North East Bus Museum at the former Springwell Bankfoot Locomotive shed on the original part of the Bowes Railway in Tyne and Wear.

The North East Bus Preservation Society members run a working museum for public transport vehicles, especially those from the North East of England. The Society also organises the annual August Bank Holiday Historic Vehicle Display at Seaburn Recreation Park, Sunderland.

The vehicle is seen outside the finishing shop at the Charles Roe works on the sad occasion of the Leeds factory's closure in September 1984.

DEK 3D

CHASSIS	LEYLAND TITAN PD2	1966
BODY	MASSEY	1966
TYPE	64-SEAT FORWARD ENTRANCE	

Wigan's smart maroon and white livery makes for good pictures on bright sunny days and the Massey body on this example makes a pleasant change from other Lancashire builders!

Wigan Corporation had an unusual tramway system in that it operated both standard and narrow gauge electric trams due to its municipalisation of two tramway companies. Its first electric tram ran on 25th January 1901 on a narrow gauge route, the first standard gauge electric tram running to Orrell on 26th July 1904.

Wigan's first motor bus service started on 9th June 1919 using two Pagefield single-deck buses made by Walker Brothers (Wigan) Ltd.

On 7th May 1925 the narrow gauge trams on the Martland Mill service were replaced with four Straker-Clough trolley omnibuses supplied by Clough, Smith & Co Ltd, the well-known contractors.

The last standard-gauge tramcar ran on 28th March 1931 and the four trolleybuses were withdrawn on 30th September 1931 after which the motor bus reigned supreme. A fleet of Leyland Titan TD1 double-deck buses was purchased for the tramway replacements with bodywork being built for them by three Wigan bodybuilders, Massey Bros, Northern Counties and Santus. Others were fitted with Leyland bodywork, all having low-height bodies.

After the war a large fleet of Leyland PD1 double-deck buses with Leyland lowbridge bodies entered service in the 1946-9 period (see page 79) being followed by 30 Leyland PD2/1s with Leyland highbridge bodies in 1950.

After Leyland discontinued the manufacture of bodywork in 1953 Wigan purchased its bodies from the two remaining bodybuilders in Wigan, Northern Counties and Massey Bros.

Following the 1st April 1974 local government reforms which created the Greater Manchester Metropolitan County Council, and SELNEC was renamed GMPTE to reflect its new operating area, the bus activities of Wigan Corporation became part of the new Executive. Wigan's fleet of Leylands, all with locally-built bodies passed to GMPTE's fleet.

Interestingly Northern Counties took over the Massey business in 1967 and NCME became associated with, and then owned by, GMPTE until 1986 when it was sold to its management. In 1995 Northern Counties was bought by Henleys, a group which also owns Plaxton.

A number of Wigan Corporation's buses have survived into preservation. Amongst these, and seen here, is No. 140, DEK 3D, new in December 1966, which became GMPTE No. 3281 after April 1974. Number 140 was a Leyland PD2/37 with a Massey 64-seat body.

It was withdrawn by the PTE in 1983 and in August 1983 was sold to the Wallace Driver Training School in London which used it until December 1991 when D. Cattimore of Moulden purchased it for restoration. After it obtained a full PCV Class 6 in April 1995 it became available for private hire in the full Wigan colours of maroon and white and is operated as 'DEK Travel' reflecting its origin. It is seen in April 1995 at Cobham.

If there was a typical municipal double-decker bus in the days of rear-entrance models, from the late 'twenties until the late 'sixties, it was probably a Leyland-bodied Leyland Titan. At one stage in the post-war period Leyland cheekily advertised that over 90% of British municipalities operated Leylands, even though some fleets might only have included an odd one. Nevertheless the point was valid in that Leylands were very popular and could be found operating widely throughout the British Isles.

This lowbridge Leyland-bodied Titan, dating from March 1940, is a representative of the TD7 model as introduced in October 1939, the month after war broke out. Yet it was by no means a 'wartime' type in the utility bus idiom, being an attempt to gild the lily of the previous highly successful TD5 with its smooth-running 8.6-litre engine by adding a flexible engine mounting and other revisions in design to make it even more refined. Unfortunately these included a heavy flywheel which had the unwanted side-effect of making gear-changes decidedly slow, and made the model unpopular in some fleets. This example gave fifteen years' service in Wigan and was then operated by the South Notts Bus Company of Gotham, Nottinghamshire, a company recently taken over by Nottingham City Transport Ltd. It continued to be used for several years as a staff bus.

The longevity of Leyland's metal-framed bodywork built in the famous South Works to the design introduced by Colin Bailey in 1936 is legendary. When Leyland ceased to build bus bodies in 1953 there was a great sadness coupled to a sense of loss that a fine engineering tradition had come to an end. Many of the bodies built in the period up to 1942 achieved over 20 years of service carrying the public, as in this case, despite unavoidable wartime neglect and without more than minor attention.

Post-war examples, modified only in detail despite being based on the new PD1 and PD2 chassis, often seemed well on the way to following suit but many had their careers cut short when rear-entrance double-deckers seating 53 or 56 and needing a crew of two were rendered obsolete by the new vehicle types of the 1960s. Many were sold off for non-public use or to small operators and others were exported.

Ironically, not very many products of Leyland's body department have survived into preservation. Those acquired after periods of use extending after their normal lives, owned by concerns which simply ran them into the ground, were often in very poor condition and beyond saving.

In 1969 the example shown was purchased for the West of England Transport Collection and shortly afterwards passed to the Wigan Transport Society which restored it into Wigan livery. By 1983 Tony Blackman, a prolific preservationist, had acquired it, adding it to the post-war example he also then owned. It spent time in the Tameside Transport Collection at Ashton and after changing hands again has been bought by Tony's son, Scott, who hopes to return it to the pristine condition in which it is seen here, at Brighton, in the early 'seventies.

Now in its 56th year this bus highlights perhaps better than most the problems which can face a preserved vehicle as its owner's circumstances change over the passing years, and changes of ownership become a regular fact of life.

Another Wigan vehicle to survive is seen opposite, standing behind the Wallasey Atlantean. Number 9, NEK 9K, which was new in July 1972 and became GMPTE No. 3338 after April 1974, is one of ten Atlantean type AN68 with Northern Counties bodywork seating 79.

It was withdrawn in November 1985 and in February 1987 was sold to the South Anston dealer, Kirkby, but was not collected by the time the Wigan Transport Group acquired it in May 1988. It is now kept at the St. Helens Transport Museum.

```
┌─────────────────────────────────────────────┐
│  ███████ ██   ██ ███████     ██   ██  ███████ │
│  FHF 451                                      │
└─────────────────────────────────────────────┘
```

CHASSIS	LEYLAND ATLANTEAN	1958
BODY	MCW	1958
TYPE	77-SEAT FRONT ENTRANCE	

The first of a new type to be placed in service is always regarded as something special and this Wallasey Atlantean is no exception. When an operator also recognises the importance of the vehicle that is even more useful since it will often be given special attention.

On 30th March 1901 the seven horse-drawn trams and 78 horses of the Wallasey United Tramway and Omnibus Company Ltd were purchased by Wallasey Corporation which then reconstructed and electrified the system before introducing an electric tram service on 17th March 1902.

Motor buses were first introduced in 1920 on a route linking Seacombe Ferry, Liscard and Wallasey Village, the first six buses fleet Nos. 1-6 being supplied by AEC Ltd with 32-seat single-deck bus bodies built by Hora.

At that time Wallasey Corporation was one of the few authorities which registered motor vehicles (classified as motor cars or heavy motor cars) with registrations ending in an odd number. Motor cycles and motorised bicycles had registration numbers ending with an even number.

Even after the 1921 Road Traffic Act Wallasey continued this practice – until October 1934 when the last odd number, HF 9999, was reached. It then started issuing even numbers from HF 4402 to any vehicle until HF 9998 was reached when the next series AHF 1 commenced.

It confuses many historians that most authorities prior to the 1921 Act issued two series of registration numbers, one for motor cycles and one for motor cars. There could thus be two vehicles on the road at the same time with the same registration number, with certain authorities re-issuing old numbers when the previous bearer of the mark was broken up or left the country!

Wallasey abandoned its first tram route on 19th January 1929 and its last on 30th November 1933.

The Wallasey Corporation Motors fleet of motor buses included many unusual buses such as the Karrier JKL with side panels which could be removed for fine weather passengers on the promenade at New Brighton. This was followed by a fleet of Hall Lewis bodied Karrier three-axle motor buses which arrived in 1927 and 1928, the trams being replaced with 36 Leyland Titan model TD1 low-height double-deck buses.

Wallasey Corporation was absorbed by Merseyside PTE on 1st December 1969 when Wallasey and Birkenhead became the Wirral Division of the PTE.

Wallasey was the first operator to place in service, on 8th December, 1958, one of the new rear-engined buses built by Leyland Motors which was called the 'Atlantean'. The first production model, Wallasey Fleet No. 1, was displayed at the 1958 Commercial Motor Show and was fitted with a 77-seat body built by Metro-Cammell Weymann and carried registration No. FHF 451.

It was withdrawn from service by MPTE in 1976 and stored at the Edge Lane works, Liverpool until 1979 when it was donated to the 201 Group for preservation. Restoration started in November 1979 and was nearly complete when the Group was renamed the 201 Restoration Group in 1984, the members being mostly staff of Merseyside PTE. The restored vehicle is now resplendent in the Wallasey livery of primrose green and cream and carries the Wallasey Corporation Motors legend.

MAXIMUM PERMISSABLE PSV DIMENSIONS

	Type	Length	Width	Height
1930 Road Traffic Act (effective 1931/32)	2-axle single-deck	27ft 6in	7ft 6in	10ft 6in
	3-axle single-deck	30ft 0in	7ft 6in	10ft 6in
	3-axle double-deck	30ft 0in	7ft 6in	15ft 0in
	2-axle double-deck	26ft 0in	7ft 6in	15ft 0in
1/7/1946	all vehicles		8ft 0in*	
1/6/1950	2-axle single-deck	30ft 0in	8ft 0in	10ft 6in
	2-axle double-deck	27ft 0in	8ft 0in	15ft 0in
1/6/1956	2-axle single-deck	30ft 0in	8ft 0in	
	2-axle double-deck	30ft 0in	8ft 0in	15ft 0in
07/1961	2-(or multi-axle) single-deck	36ft 0in	8ft 2½in	
	2-(or multi-axle) double-deck	36ft 0in	8ft 2½in	15ft 0in
09/1967	2-(or multi-axle) single-deck	12m (39ft 4in)	8ft 2½in	
	2-(or multi-axle) double-deck	12m (39ft 4in)	8ft 2½in	15ft 0in

Subject to Traffic Commissioners approval for use on permitted roads only

NEXT IN THIS SERIES –

This new series from Venture Publications combines an attractive pictorial record with background information which is not merely interesting but, in many cases, difficult to find. The series will become an invaluable reference library in itself.

The next Volume of preserved vehicles will cover a selection from the former BET fleets – from Aldershot & District to Western Welsh in alphabetical terms. Available from transport bookshops or our Mail Order Department during Summer 1996.

REGISTRATION MARKS

The UK registration system became operative from 1903 and initially used a system of letters followed by numbers, with a maximum of six characters on the plate.

Around 1953 the major Motor Taxation Offices had exhausted their supply of letters and a new system was instigated whereby the numbers were put before the letters. Some smaller authorities never needed to change to the numbers first system.

By 1962 a further change was seen to be needed and a system of suffix letters was introduced in 1963, working through the alphabet and using most but not all letters, on a sequential annual basis. By 1965 all authorities were using this system which lasted until 1983.

This system had used all the available letters by 1983 and the current system of prefix letters was introduced from that time.

In 1974, following the boundary changes, many registration letters were re-allocated to other areas, thus breaking the continuity which had existed from the beginning of the system in 1903. For a full explanation of the various changes and a list of all registration letter allocations we recommend interested readers to purchase a copy of one of the two specialist books on the subject.

Motor Vehicle Registration Marks of the British Isles, by Bowden and Watts price £3.95 gives a brief concise listing whilst *Registration Plates of the World*, by Parker, Weeks and Wilson is the definitive work on the subject priced at £15.99.

Both these paperback books are available from the MDS mail order department at 128, Pikes Lane, Glossop Derbyshire.